Planning Competences

ICB4 Reference Guide

Planning Competences

ICB4 Reference Guide

Legal Address:
International Project Management Association (IPMA)
c/o Maurer&Stäger AG, Fraumünsterstrasse 17, Postfach 318, 8024 Zürich, Switzerland

Planning Competences, ICB4 Reference Guide, version 1. is a standard accepted by 70 countries.

ISBN Hardcopy: 9789401812610
ISBN eBook: 9789401812627
ISBN ePub: 9789401812634

Publisher: Van Haren Publishing, 's-Hertogenbosch - The Netherlands
www.vanharen.net

Editor:
Agnes Roux-Kiener

Table of Content

Foreword

As IPMA celebrates its 60th anniversary, we reflect on its remarkable journey and reaffirm its founding mission: to enhance the competences of individuals in Project Management. Over six decades, IPMA has cultivated a global network of practitioners, fostering collaboration with corporations, government agencies, academic institutions, training organizations and consulting firms. These partnerships have enabled IPMA to create and disseminate globally recognized competence standards. Through these standards, project management professionals from diverse cultures and regions are empowered to learn, grow and drive progress for their organisations and stakeholders.

This commitment to advancing the field is embodied in the Planning Competences - ICB4 Reference Guide. Derived from the comprehensive IPMA Individual Competence Baseline (ICB4), it serves as a pivotal resource for Project Planning Professionals. It focuses on equipping them with the competences necessary for their critical role in collaborating with Project Managers to achieve project success. Far from being a traditional manual on Project Management, this Guide addresses the specific needs of Project Planning Professionals. It offers a pathway to acquire the knowledge, skills and abilities required to excel in their roles, advancing both their careers and the discipline as a whole.

The creation of this Guide is a testament to the dedication of a global community of experts. IPMA extends its heartfelt gratitude to the editorial team and contributors from around the world, whose invaluable feedback enriched every stage of this Guide's development. The collaborative efforts across vast distances and multiple time zones stand as a shining example of what can be achieved through shared vision and teamwork.

As you engage with this Guide, we invite you to join us in celebrating not only IPMA's storied past but also its vibrant present and promising future. Together, we continue to elevate the practice of Project Management, fostering a community where learning, sharing and collaboration are at the forefront of progress.

Signatures:

Mladen Vukomanović, IPMA President	Jose Reyes, IPMA VP Standards, Qualifications & Products	Agnes Roux-Kiener, Editor of the Project Planner, ICB4 Reference Guide

Introduction

This document is derived from the IPMA Individual Competence Baseline (ICB4) that is a global Standard for Project Management. Just like in ICB4, Project Planning competences are structured into three competence categories:

- The Perspective competences dealing with the context and the environment of a project
- The People competences dealing with personal behaviours and social topics
- The Practice competences dealing with the construction and management of a project plan

This document covers the Perspective competences and their key competence indicators. These are the same as for Project managers (refer to ICB4) but their descriptions are tailored for Project Planning managers in order to help them understand the relevance of these competences for their profession.
The five Perspective competence elements are described first in this document and are numbered from 1.1 to 1.5 (these numbers are also used in the Project Planner self-assessment document).

1.1 Strategy
1.2 Governance, Structure and Process
1.3 Compliance, Standards and Regulations
1.4 Power and Interest
1.5 Culture and Values

For People competences, as all people working on projects should be driven by the same behavioural competences, the competences described in the ICB4 will be used. Free download of the IPMA ICB4 document is available through this page (click on download eBook): https://shop.ipma.world/shop/ipma-standards/books-ipma-standards/individual-competence-baseline-for-project-management/?v=11aedd0e4327
The 10 People competence elements included in ICB4 are numbered from 4.4.1 to 4.4.10 in ICB4 and from 2.1 to 2.10 in the Planner self-assessment document:

2.1 Self-Reflection and Self-Management
2.2 Personal Integrity and Reliability
2.3 Personal Communication
2.4 Relationships and Engagement
2.5 Leadership
2.6 Teamwork
2.7 Conflicts and Crises
2.8 Resourcefulness
2.9 Negotiation
2.10 Results orientation

This document also includes Practice competences that have been tailored to the planning profession. The 13 Practice competence elements for planning are described in second part of this document and are numbered from 3.1 to 3.13 (numbers also used in the Project Planner self-assessment document).

3.1 Project Planning Design and Requirements
3.2 Project Planning Organisation, Information and Communication
3.3 Contracts and Project Delays
3.4 Project Scope, Deliverables and Structure
3.5 Project Scheduling
3.6 Project Time and Milestone Management
3.7 Project Resource Allocation
3.8 Project Resource Optimization
3.9 Monitoring Project Progress
3.10 Planning Risks and Opportunities
3.11 Planning Steering and Control
3.12 Planning Stakeholders
3.13 Change / Transformation Management

In this document, for each competence element there are:

- a definition, a purpose and a description together with knowledge and skills / abilities related to this competence.
- Key Competence Indicators (KCIs) with measures so that the level of a competence of a candidate might be assessed.

This document is a reference guide for candidates who would like to develop themselves in the project planning profession. It is not a prescriptive cookbook.

Glossary of terms

Baseline plan: project plan approved (contracted). Progress of project execution is measured against baseline plan.

PBS - Product Breakdown Structure: tree shape identification of all products (both final and intermediate) and components to be produced and/or used in the project.

Plan: Description of project execution (identification of work items - work packages, activities, tasks -, project logic - links or logical relationships between identified work packages, activities and tasks -, project organisation - identification of contributors, contributions, as well as material and machine resources, project schedule and related resource profiles).

Planning: construction of the project plan (from system design to baseline plan). Planning consists in collecting data from relevant sources, analysing those and consolidating them, negotiating all adjustment needed to assure the consistency of the project plan.

RBS - Resource Breakdown Structure: tree-shaped identification of all resources (human, material and machines) contributing to the project, used during the project, and possibly generated during the project.

Schedule: project timeline consistent with other components of the project plan (identification of work items, logics, organisation and estimates).

Scheduling: construction of the project schedule. Scheduling consists of collecting data from relevant sources, analysing those and consolidating them, negotiating all adjustments needed to assure consistency of the project schedule with estimates, execution assumptions and uncertainties.

WBS - Work Breakdown Structure: tree-shaped identification of all subproject, phases, stages, work packages, activities and tasks of the project.

1 Perspective Competence Elements for Project Planning

The perspective competence elements deal with the framework within which project planning is implemented. They are the same as in the ICB4 document but this part explains their relevance to project planners.
The five perspective competences are:
1.1 Strategy
1.2 Governance, Structure and Process
1.3 Compliance, Standards and Regulation
1.4 Power and Interest
1.5 Culture and Values

1.1 Strategy

Definition

This competence element describes how planning strategies are understood and transformed for a smooth execution of the project. This is therefore about defining a performance planning management system in line with the organisation's planning strategy and vision. This ensures it is highly correlated with the mission and the sustainability of the organisation.

Purpose

The purpose of this competence element is to understand the planning strategy and strategic processes, thus enabling project, programme or portfolio to manage their project planning within the contextual aspects.

Description

This competence describes the formal justification of the project's planning goals as well as the realization of benefits for the Organisation's long-term planning goals.

This encompasses the discipline of strategic performance management in which an organisation breaks up its strategic planning goals into manageable elements in order to:

- Achieve beneficial changes in organisational culture, business systems and processes.
- Establish and pursue agreed strategic planning targets.
- Allocate and rank resources,
- Inform management of the need to change strategic planning objectives
- Stimulate continuous improvement.

Strategic plans encompass long-term visions and mid- or short-term planning strategies and should be aligned with the mission, quality policy and corporate values of organisations. This competence also includes the process of understanding the organisational environment, which develops the desired state of benefits.
Strategy alignment should therefore embed the organisation's planning strategy and vision into the project planning goals.
Throughout the strategic alignment processes, planners may apply different models for disseminating and managing of strategic planning goals (e.g., the balanced scorecard, performance matrix, environmental analyses). Thus, the planner implements a performance management system, usually run by critical performance variables, i.e., critical success factors (CSFs) and key performance indicators (KPIs). Hence, each project planning is controlled through a set of CSFs and KPIs to assure the sustainability of an organisation.

Knowledge

- Management the achievement of planning objectives
- Critical Success Factors
- Key Performance Indicators
- Organisational Vision
- Difference between tactics and planning strategy
- Interactive management and control diagnostic systems
- Strategic Performance Management
- Benchmarking
- Management control systems
- Strategic Thinktanks

Skills / abilities

- Analysis and synthesis
- Entrepreneurship
- Reflection on the organisation's planning goals
- Strategic thinking
- Sustainable thinking
- Contextual awareness
- Results orientation

KEY COMPETENCE INDICATORS

1.1.1 Align with organisation mission and vision

Description
The planner knows, reflects on, and can translate the organisation's vision and planning strategy into their project. The planner always needs to ensure that the project planning goals are in sync with the vision, quality policy and values of the organisation. If the relation between the project planning benefits and organisational purpose is vague, the planner needs to perform periodic checking of the project's planning benefits against the purpose written in formal strategy documents. The alignment is usually done by using management control systems and formal tools (e.g., critical success factors, success criteria, key performance indicators).

Measures
- Knows the planning strategy and vision of the organisation
- Aligns the project planning goals with planning vision and strategy by using diagnostic control management systems (top-down approach and pre-set planning goals)
- Controls whether the project planning objectives and benefits are in sync with the organisation's planning vision and strategy
- Develops and implements strategic planning alignment measures (e.g., critical success factors, key performance indicators)
- Checks whether the project planning is delivering benefits to the organisation

1.1.2 Identify and exploit opportunities to influence organisation strategy

Description
The planner is familiar with the planning strategy-making process, often done in a top-down approach by the organisation's management. However, intended planning strategies are often not realised if the environment changes and, while pursuing a certain path, new opportunities and risks are emerging. Therefore, the planner needs to reflect not only on the predefined strategic planning goals, but also on the tools and methods of questioning these planning goals and influencing the board to make the necessary improvements. These influences are managed through interactive control systems and by applying a bottom-up approach.

Measures
- Knows the planning strategy-making process
- Identifies new risks and opportunities which could alter the planning strategy
- Engages co-workers in questioning this planning strategy by implementing interactive control management systems (bottom-up approach and stretch planning goals)
- Identifies strategic planning improvements
- Intervenes in the strategy-making process by suggesting changes

1.1.3 Develop and ensure the ongoing validity of the business / organisational justification

Description
The planner is able to provide a formal document which states the project planning issues including the business or organisational benefits that the project plan has to deliver.
These issues should also explain integration aspects with new elements and should be the basis for the success criteria and benefits the project should deliver (the scope). The planner can participate in creating, explaining, implementing and sometimes modifying these issues that should not be static, but updated periodically and reassessed throughout the project.
In addition, the planner should constantly monitor or control the configuration, check if the project has strategically obsolete or redundant elements and perform the proper alignment, even if this means terminating the project.

Measures
- Reflects at the project planning level the business and/or organisational policy of the organisation
- Identifies planning objectives to meet the challenges set
- Validates and highlights the business policy and company organisation to the customers of the project planning
- Reassesses and validates project planning issues in a general context
- Defines and manages the configuration of the project schedule (completeness and functionality of the organisation of the project planning)
- Identifies, evaluates and reviews key success factors for project planning
- Applies issue delivery management to ensure that project planning configuration generates desired outcomes
- Analyses the need to end project planning due to redundancy or obsolescence of the planning strategy

1.1.4 Determine, assess and review critical success factors

Description
The planner is able to define, interpret and prioritize critical success factors (CSFs) which directly relate to the project and project plan. CSFs are directly connected with the organisational planning goals and to the project's business planning goals. Therefore, by achieving the project planning benefits, the organisation fulfils strategic, tactical and operational objectives, and ultimately achieves organisational success. The planner can grasp both the formal and informal context of the success factors and identify their influence on the final outcome of the project. The relative importance of success factors associated with planning may change, due to both contextual factors and the dynamics of the project itself. Personnel changes, both internal and external, may also have an influence. Therefore, the planner should periodically check and

evaluate the actuality and relative importance of the CSFs and, if necessary, make changes in order to sustain success of project, even if this means its premature end.

Measures
- Derives and/or develops a set of CSFs associated with planning
- Uses formal CSFs associated with strategic alignment planning, but also identifies their informal context
- Invites employees to consider the organisation's planning strategy when developing CSFs associated with planning (interactive management control, complementary planning objectives)
- Uses CSFs associated with project planning for strategic alignment
- Uses CSFs associated with project planning for stakeholder management
- Uses CSFs associated with project planning for developing incentives / rewards and a motivated culture
- Re-assesses the achievement of CSFs associated with project planning in a superior strategic context

1.1.5 Determine, assess and review key performance indicators

Description
The planner is able to manage related key performance indicators (KPIs) for each CSFs associated with project plan and planning activities. KPIs are the core of many strategic performance management systems and are used for measuring or indicating the fulfilment of the CSFs.
Usually, KPIs associated with project plan and planning activities are either predefined by the organisation or developed by the planner using best templates (e.g., balanced scorecard). KPIs associated with planning can be used as leading measures (preceding a strategic event or milestone), lagging measures (following a strategic event or milestone) or in real-time dashboards. Throughout the project, KPIs may change due to both contextual factors and the dynamics of the project itself. Personnel changes, both internal and external to the project, may also have an impact on KPIs. Therefore, the planner should periodical check and assess the actuality and relative importance of the KPIs and, if necessary, make the required changes to sustain the success.
KPIs should also involve soft aspects such as motivation, communication within the team, personal development of members. Which reflect the strategic planning objective, i.e., the benefit one wants to achieve.
In addition, KPIs should cover a wide range of other aspects such as adherence to certain governance processes and support functions (decision-making, reporting, acquiring resources and administrative processes), meeting standards and regulations, to comply with cultural norms and values both of the organisation and of the wider society.

Measures

- Derives and/or develops a KPI associated with planning (or a set of KPIs) for each critical success factor
- Decides on the use of leading, lagging and real-time measures when developing KPIs
- Uses KPIs for strategic performance management
- Uses KPIs to influence stakeholders
- Uses KPIs for developing personal development plans
- Uses KPIs for developing an incentive or reward system
- Re-assesses project configuration using KPIs and managing the achievement of planning objectives

1.2 Governance, Structures and Processes

Definition

This competence element defines the understanding and consideration of and the alignment with the established structures, systems and processes of the organisation that provides support for projects and influence the way they are organised, implemented and managed.
The governance, structures and processes of an organisation may comprise both temporary systems (such as projects) and permanent systems (such as programme and portfolio management systems, financial/administrative systems, supporting systems, reporting systems, and decision-making and auditing systems)
Sometimes, these systems can even form a strategic reason for a project; for example, when a project is initiated for the purpose of improving business processes or establishing new systems.

Purpose

The purpose of this competence element is to enable the planner to effectively participate in and consider the impact of governance, structures and processes and project planning.

Description

Structures and processes are an essential part of the governance system of any organisation. Aligning with structures and processes means the ability to utilize value systems, roles and responsibilities, processes and policies established in an organisation to ensure that projects achieve their objectives and strategic corporate goals. To plan projects in line with the established organisational structures and processes requires a basic understanding of the various types of initiatives and our project-oriented organisation works, as well as the benefits associated with management by projects. It includes the alignment with the permanent processes related to the management of the projects. Most project-oriented organisations are various types of supporting structures and processes for projects. In the domain of project management, the individual may be called upon to provide data and business intelligence to the governance process and to work within existing structures and processes. Some projects may result in changes to structures and processes.
Examples of supporting structures and processes are found in line functions such as human resources (HR), finance and control, and information technology (IT). Major project organisations may also provide more dedicated support to project management through a project management office (PMO). To be competent in structures and processes also means the ability to review and apply feedback and lessons learned from previous projects.

Knowledge

- Basic principles and characteristics of project management
- Basics of Portfolio Management
- Basics of Programme Management
- Organisational Design Basics
- Formal organisation and informal relationships of project, programme and portfolio management
- Governance
- Organisational theories and contract management

Skills / abilities

- Leadership
- Reporting, monitoring and control
- Planning and communication
- Design thinking

KEY COMPETENCE INDICATORS

1.2.1 Know the principles of project management and the way they are implemented

Description

The planner reflects on the concept of the project and management by projects and can clarify the difference between different types of organisations settings (e.g., functional metrics and project-oriented organisation) come up and knows how to optimally align performance with the current organisational setting. The planner can explain the characteristics and principles on which management by project is based and is able to set up project-oriented environment. Furthermore, the planner is aware of the maturity concept of the project-oriented organisations covering organisational competences, project and programme competences, and individual competences.

Measures

- Knows how to identify a project and knows the principles of project management
- Explains the characteristics of functional, project-oriented or matrix-oriented organisations, and takes them into account about planning
- Explains and applies the concept of project planning
- Identifies and implements planning by considering project management concepts within the organisation
- Explains and identifies the current maturity level of an organisation

1.2.2 Know and apply the principles of programme management and the way they are implemented

Description
If the project is part of a programme, the planner has to align the project with the programme plan and planning activities. The planner also has to know how the principles of programme plan management are implemented in the specific organisation.
The dependencies between the project and the programme as well as between the different projects within the programme have to be analysed in terms of input, goals, outcomes. Dealing with those dependencies means setting up and maintaining interfaces between the project and the programme.

Measures
- Knows how to identify a programme
- Knows the principles of programme management
- Explains the characteristics of programme planning (planning objectives, input/output data, results)

1.2.3 Know and apply portfolio planning principles and the way they are implemented

Description
The planner knows the way in which portfolio planning management is implemented into specific permanent organisation. Therefore, the individual knows the portfolio criteria and required inputs and outputs and identifies the impact on the project planning on the portfolio. The planner is able to discover different constraints within the portfolio and can take these constraints into account to harmonise resource actualization of their project. The planner is able to filter and/or funnel the communication channels with the respective portfolio in order to positively influence the project performance. The planner knows the vertical (e.g., with the programme manager or programme steering committee) and horizontal (e.g., with individual in the programme-other project teams) lines of communication as part of the overall coordination process with the programme or portfolio.

Measures
- Knows how to identify a portfolio
- Knows the principles of portfolio management
- Explains the characteristics of portfolio planning - critical success factors (CSFs) and key performance indicators (KPIs)
- Familiar with the concept of portfolio planning management (organisational structures and processes)
- Communicates successfully within a respective portfolio plan in order to successfully manage a project plan

1.2.4 Align the project with supporting functions

Description
Project supporting functions (a project office, a project management office -PMO- or similar) provide multifaceted support to the project and/or the planner responsible for it (organisation, planning, reporting, meeting management, documentation.). To ensure the necessary support from the project supporting function, the planner has to know relevant contact people within the project supporting function and how to establish and maintain good relationships with them.

Measures
- Knows the people, processes, and services related to supporting functions
- Uses the organisation's project supporting functions for effective project planning support
- Establishes and maintains relationships with supporting functions
- Enforces hierarchical communication rules in the organisation using specific tools and methods

1.2.5 Align the project with the organisations' decision-making and reporting structures and quality requirements

Description
The success of a project plan and planning activities is highly dependent on the right decisions made at the right level of the organisation at the right time. Every decision should be prepared, presented, accepted, recorded, communicated and finally implemented. Formal and informal routines and special rules for decision-making beyond the individual's authority and responsibility exist in each organisation. Therefore, the planner requires knowledge on the decision-making structure and processes and ability to structure and manage the project accordingly. Periodic reporting on the actual status is essential for trust by its stakeholders to assure traceability of the progress. Different project stakeholders can have different information needs (type of information, delivery method, frequency of reports) that the planner must consider.
The parent organisation can have different forms of quality assurance which relate to projects (organisation, project, finance, technical, security). It is important for the planner to take this into account when developing the quality plan for their project plan, to decide which parts of the project plan should be put under quality assurance and to know that the project team members should be involved in the quality assurance activities.

Measures
- Identifies standard rules and specific rules of planning organisation for decision-making outside of its competence and responsibility
- Aligns planning communication with the needs of the temporary and permanent organisations

- Applies the organisation's reporting procedures to project planning using specific tools and methods
- Applies the organisation's quality system when setting up the planning-related information system within the permanent organisation

1.2.6 Align the project with human resources processes and functions

Description
The Human Resources function provides the project team with multifaceted support in terms of temporary employment, training, salary, motivation, stress, well-being, ethics and management of assignments (arrivals and exits).
A good relationship with the human resources department and the consideration of the applicable processes in this area may increase the influence on resource availability and quality in terms of adequate authorities.
To provide the necessary support to the human resources functions, the planner must establish and maintain relationships with their contact at the relevant structure.

Measures
- Uses human resources functions to establish staff with the skills required by planning
- Manages interfaces between temporary planning organisation and human resources functions
- Establishes and maintains relationships with human resources functions
- Uses human resources processes to provide training and individual development related to planning

1.2.7 Align the project with finance and control processes and functions

Description
The finance and control function of an organisation is often established as a line function providing mandatory rules, procedures and guidelines. Knowing these rules and how to utilize them effectively and efficiently are crucial for the planner for successful funding, monitoring and/or reporting on financial topics.
The finance and control function of an organisation often serves as a support function, offering a variety of utility functions for the planner such as how to apply for, justify, manage and report on financial resources and how to manage, administer, distribute, monitor and manage finances.
The planner needs to know various financial models for funding (e.g., public, private, public-private partnerships, subsidies, commercial.) endorsed by the permanent organisation. To ensure the necessary support from the finance and control functions, the planner can benefit from establishing and maintaining relationships with the relevant contacts in the finance and control function.

Measures

- Integrates financial and control processes into planning
- Differentiates mandatory and optional financial constraints from financial and control functions and takes them into account in planning
- Monitors and controls whether rules and other guidelines are effectively considered in planning

1.3 Compliance, standards and regulation

Definition

This competence element describes how the planner interprets and integrates internal and external constraints in each sector such as a country, company or industry. Compliance is the process of ensuring adequate adherence to a given set of norms. Compliance requirements operate on a spectrum from voluntary an informal to mandatory and formal.
Standards, norms, regulations and legislation have an impact on project planning and define how they must be organized, managed and planned to be feasible and effective. These rules describe requirements related to contracts and agreements, intellectual property and patents, health, safety, security, environmental protection and professional standards.
These rules also describe the data use and protection requirements associated with users and stakeholders.

Purpose

The purpose of this competence element is to enable the planner:

- to consider and manage the integration of these rules into a plan,
- to measure their relevance to the codes of the organisation and the whole society,
- and to improve their approach.

Description

Projects face different restrictions and requirements related to the development of a product or service as part of the project management and production processes. These constraints and requirements correspond to the geographical, social and professional specificities of the project and its external environment in the form of laws, standards and regulations.
Before launching a project, the planner must analyse the scope and configuration of the project and look for relevant rules that will have a direct or indirect influence on the plan. These rules should be seen as potential risks and opportunities for management. Compliance with them may have an impact on the organisational culture, structures and processes. In the field of project management, the planner may have to integrate these rules into the project planning process.
This competence element includes benchmarking and improving project planning skills in the organisation. Developing these skills is a process of continuous improvement of the organisation and the duty of each individual. This involves learning and improving planning strategies to influence project management cultures.
The planner should use this skill to demonstrate how the management system can be improved. By increasing the competence of project, programme or portfolio planning,

the organisation increases its ability to choose, carry out and succeed in its strategic choices, and therefore ensuring the sustainability of the organisation.

Knowledge

- Legislation applicable to plan
- Professional regulations applicable to plan
- Project management rules and standards (IPMA standard)
- ISO standards (ISO 21500 - relating to project management - or other ISO/TC258 standards)
- Principles of sustainable development applicable to plan
- Benchmarking theories
- Benchmarking tools and methods
- Knowledge Management
- Ethics
- Rules of business conduct
- Legal concepts

Skills / abilities

- Critical thinking
- Benchmarking analysis
- Adaptation of standards to specific bodies
- Communication on standards and regulations
- Management by example

KEY COMPETENCE INDICATORS

1.3.1 Identify and ensure that the project complies with all applicable legislation

Description
The planner knows the legal policies of an organisation and is able to implement them in the project plan as well as in the project planning activities. In addition, the planner knows which parts of the legal regulations (civil, criminal, labour, intellectual property) and which good practices are applicable in the project planning.
The planner must ensure that the project planning is carried out in accordance with the law and must be able to identify or know which tasks have particular legal requirements and which legal obligations apply.
The planner is able to identify the legal requirements that need to be taken into account and therefore knows the formal procedures to obtain advice from specialists able to provide the corresponding relevant information.

The planner is aware of the requirements of regulatory bodies in relation to project planning, how these requirements can be met and what audit procedures should be applied.

Measures

- Identifies the legal context and its impact on plan
- Analyses the legislation applicable to plan
- Identifies policy planning risks to consider and consults with experts
- Recognises and treats regulatory bodies as planning stakeholders

1.3.2 Identify and ensure that the project complies with all relevant health, safety, security and environmental regulations (HSSE)

Description

The planner is aware about the health, safety, security and environmental (H.S.S.E.) regulations applicable to the project plan and planning activities. In addition, the planner is able to recognise any potential issues regarding the H.S.S.E. that require special attention.
The planner is able to determine how the activities or products of the project may have an impact on the project plan and the users of the final product and applies if necessary H.S.S.E. protection measures.

Measures

- Identifies H.S.S.E. rules applicable to project plan
- Defines the H.S.S.E. context for project plan
- Identifies the risks arising from the implementation of H.S.S.E. measures in the project
- Provides and schedules tasks associated with a safe, secure and healthy environment for project team members
- Plans the tasks associated with the H.S.S.E. to meet the requirements of sustainable development

1.3.3 Identify and ensure that the project complies with all relevant codes of conduct and professional regulation

Description

The planner should be able to identify relevant professional regulations in the context of project planning. It should identify specific codes of conduct (ethical standards written in official documents) and business practices that may sometimes be prescribed by law. In addition, these rules are often directly related to procurement procedures and may present a high risk to a project if they have not been identified.

Measures

- Considers the codes applicable to commercial relations in plan
- Knows the professional regulations applied to the industrial sector in which they work (public administration, civil engineering, information technology, telecommunications)
- Identifies and takes into account commercial uses, even if not written
- Brings procurement practices into line with business rules and practices

1.3.4 Identify and ensure that the project complies with relevant sustainability principles and objectives

Description

The planner complies with the guidelines and rules concerning sustainable development in the organisation and for the wider society. The planner is able to achieve a viable balance between the requirements of society, the impacts on the eco-environment and the economy. The planner understands that the aspects of sustainable development (measures and attitudes) often vary according to the countries and cultures concerned. The planner integrates economic, social and environmental aspects to meet the sustainable development requirements for project plan and the resulting products.

Measures

- Defines and communicates planning objectives related to sustainable development
- Aligns planning objectives with organisational sustainability planning strategies
- Plans W.P. and sustainability tasks

1.3.5 Assess, use and develop professional standards and tools for the project

Description

The planner is able to comply with and use professional standards. Good project management practices are a combination of international standards and the tools and methods the planner has personally developed. Based on this, the planner selects appropriate tools, methods and concepts (project process, stakeholder management, risk management).

The planner therefore always tries to find the best approach for project planning by using professional standards and adding and developing new approaches.

Measures

- Identifies and uses professional standards related to planning
- Identifies the specifics of a standard and manages the risks and opportunities arising from applying a standard to project planning
- Identifies and uses best practices for project planning

1.3.6 Assess, benchmark and improve the organisational project management competence

Description

Benchmarking is a continuous improvement process that involves comparing the organisation's project planning processes to those identified as good practices. In this way, the planner seeks to develop project planning skills.

Good practices can often be identified as those applicable in mature organisations globally. Usually, these organisations are internationally recognised and have been awarded for their performance in project management (for example, as part of IPMA Project Excellence awards).

The goal of the benchmarking process is to advance project planning by acquiring the know-how of a mature organisation.

Organisational benchmarking often follows a progressive maturity or organisational competence model defining what individual structures, processes, methods, and competences an organisation must have to achieve a certain level of maturity or category of competence.

Benchmarking can be done on an internal basis (comparison of different projects within an organisation), a competitive basis (compared to an organisation that is a direct competitor that is often difficult to confront), or a functional or generic basis (compared to a non-competing organisation).

The planner always tries to improve project planning in a way that contributes to the organisation's strategic planning goals. Improvements can be defined and implemented in agreement with central services.

In addition, the planner is able to identify the processes and structures associated with project management (PMO) and is able and willing to make or propose organisational improvements. Finally, the improvements made are communicated to the whole organisation.

Measures

- Identifies and evaluates or participates in the identification and assessment of weaknesses in organisational competence in project planning
- Identifies and prepares or participates in the identification and preparation of relevant benchmarking for these weaknesses
- Identifies or participates in the identification of benchmarks and good practices targeted
- Conducts or participates in benchmarking between current performance and planning best practices
- Identifies or participates in the identification of necessary improvement measures
- Implements or participates in the implementation of identified measures and evaluates the benefits gained
- Disseminates or participates in the dissemination of the know-how acquired through the organisation of the project

1.4 Power and Interest

Definition

This competence element includes identifying, analysing, engaging and managing the attitudes and expectations of all relevant stakeholders. Planners, groups or organisations participating in, affecting, being affected by, or interested in the execution or the result of the project plan should be seen as stakeholders. This may include sponsors, customers and users, suppliers / subcontractors, alliances, partners and also other projects, programmes or portfolios. Stakeholder engagement includes constantly revising, monitoring and acting upon their interests and influence on project planning. It can also result in the development of strategic alliances to build organisational capacities and capabilities where both risks and reward are shared.

Purpose

The purpose of this competency element is to enable the planner to identify and effectively manage stakeholder interests, influence and expectations.

Description

Stakeholder engagement is an ongoing process, throughout the project lifecycle. Stakeholders are the partners for and through whom the project planning will be successful. Stakeholders' expectations, needs and ideas form the basis for the project; stakeholders are the necessary contributors to the project in terms of money and resources; they are also the users of the project outcome.

Stakeholders come in various forms and groupings (higher management, users, suppliers, partners, operators, pressure and special interest groups.) They have varying attitudes, influences, and interests. Therefore, each stakeholder or group of stakeholders has different information needs.

An engagement strategy (often laid down in a communication plan) is therefore essential. This strategy might be executed by setting up formal and informal communication channels, as well as more involving forms, such as alliances, collaboration or networks. Alliances are often documented and formalized through a contractual document such as an alliance contract, or through the creation of a joint venture entity. Employees often work in separate parts within an entity or may be part of one or more different organisations. Networks have no clear power structure, and are therefore more difficult to engage with.

Changes in the stakeholder environment must be continuously monitored to ensure that objectives are met.

Knowledge

- Stakeholder interests
- Stakeholder influence
- Stakeholder Engagement Strategy
- Communication plan
- Collaborative agreements and alliances
- External environment scanning relating to social, political, economic and technological developments

Skills / abilities

- Stakeholders' identification
- Analysis of contextual pressures
- Demonstrating strategic communication skills
- Expectations management
- Formal and informal communication
- Good presentation skills
- Networking skills to identify potentially useful and opposite stakeholders
- Contextual awareness
- Undertaking conflict resolution

KEY COMPETENCE INDICATORS

1.4.1 Assess the personal ambitions and interests of others and the potential impact of these on the project

Description

The planner identifies all the people, groups, and organisations relevant to project planning. The planner must first analyse the attitudes of each of the stakeholders (individual or group) and identify the reasons for their attitude (interests in the outcomes or in the process of the project). Next, the planner must understand what beneficial or harmful effect (influence) this stakeholder (individual or group) can potentially have on the project planning.

Stakeholders' interests may come from different sources (for example, because they want, or must, use project deliverables or because they compete for scarce resources or budget). These interests can be large or modest, positive or negative. In the latter case, they reflect opposition to the project, for one reason or another. The influence of a stakeholder can be greater or smaller and can apply to one or more areas (such as being able to provide or deny funding, resources, office space and equipment, priority, access). The planner performs an analysis at the beginning of each project, identifying the stakeholders, their interests and influence. During the project, the planner maintains an active analysis of the project environment, to identify new stakeholders, changed interests or changed influences. These changes in the stakeholder environment may be the result of changes in the project itself (for example, moving from a design phase to an execution phase). More often, they are the result of changes in the context of the project (organisational changes, personnel changes in management, economic changes, new regulations.). The planner analyses the relevance of these changes to project planning.

Measures

- Identifies the main categories of stakeholders in the project plan and planning activities
- Identifies and qualifies stakeholder interests in the project
- Identifies and evaluates the influence of stakeholders
- Identifies relevant changes in or around the project
- Analyses the consequences of changes for the project
- Takes actions to manage project stakeholders

1.4.2 Assess the informal influence of individuals and groups and its potential impact on the project

Description

Informal influence has to be distinguished from formal influences laid out in organisational documents and processes. People may have influence for many reasons and through many different means. Apart from the formally agreed on legitimate power (e.g., of department heads, executives, judges and school teachers) there are many other bases of power, for instance coercive, reward, referent, and expert power. Relations are a strong base of power, too. Influencing decisions through use of personal relations is a common and often effective way. There is often a marked difference in the ability people or groups to influence certain kinds of decisions, or decisions taken in a specific knowledge area or part of the organisation (its 'reach' or influence). Every person and group influence has its own reach, and it is important to know that reach.

Measures

- Acknowledges and can estimate the influence, power and reach of certain individuals in various settings
- Is able to discern group affiliation s and relations in relation with the project plan and planning activities

1.4.3 Assess the personalities and working styles of others and employ them to the benefit of the project

Description

Everybody is unique, and will act and operate in their own specific way. Style is also influenced by cultural factors, as discussed in "Culture and values". Different people may have the same ambitions and/or interests, yet may use different style in using their influence. Other people may display the same behaviour or style, yet differ in ambitions and/or interests. The planner has to acknowledge the differences while working with individuals and groups in an effective and efficient way.

Measures

- Identifies and acknowledges the differences between behavioural style and personality
- Identifies and acknowledges the differences between cultural style and personality

1.5 Culture and Values

Definition

This competence element defines how the planner integrates their mission into the culture and values of the organisation and the wider society. It also discusses the influence that the planner involved in managing a project can have on the culture and values conveyed by that project. It also deals with the consideration of changes or transformations in project planning.
Culture may be defined as a set of related behaviours within a community and the importance that individuals attach to it. Values may be defined as a set of concepts on which community members base their actions. These values may include codes of ethics. Many organisations explicitly describe the corporate values in their strategy.

Purpose

The purpose of this competence element is to enable the planner to recognise and integrate the influence of internal and external cultural parameters on the project: approach, planning objectives, process, sustainability of the results obtained and acceptability of these results.

Description

Organisations are social systems where personal behaviour is integrated into a social framework of values, visions, norms, symbols, beliefs, habits, shared goals: i.e., a culture. This culture has explicit origins and formal aspects (such as the stated mission of the organisation and the company's values), as well as more implicit informal aspects (beliefs, common practices). In addition, every organisation acts in a society which also has a specific culture with values, norms, symbols, beliefs, habits. All these cultural aspects affect how people and projects interact with each other as well as with stakeholders. Projects are often an integral part of the organisation. However, while being temporary organisations they need to align their internal culture with the culture of their environment (external adaptation and internal integration).
In the field of project management, the planner may have to position the project planning in relation to the culture of the organisation and the corresponding values.
In a multicultural project, the planner may have to deal with multiple standards of cultures and values. These aspects are key for projects involving different companies, organisations or groups, thus forming a multicultural environment. At the start of a project, and then periodically, the planner should identify the different cultures implemented in the internal and external context of the project and the organisation. They must apply this approach in order to achieve the planning goals and objectives in the most effective and efficient manner.
If available, the results of research into standards, internal or external, regulations or guidelines (principles of governance, codes of conduct) may bring these different

cultures into consistency. Projects are sometimes explicitly carried out to change the culture and change the values of an organisation. Return of experience at the end of a project may improve the cultural approach in future projects.

Knowledge

- Relevant cultural aspects, values, norms and behaviours
- Mission and organisational vision
- Framing of the mission
- Company values and policies
- Quality policies
- Ethics
- Corporate Social Responsibility
- Theories on culture

Skills / abilities

- Values awareness
- Cultural awareness
- Respect for other cultures and values
- Working in different cultural environments
- Dealing with issues related to cultural aspects

KEY COMPETENCE INDICATORS

1.5.1 Assess the culture and values of the society and their implications for the project

Description

All projects are embedded in a society (sometimes even in more than one society). The company's values and unwritten rules can deeply influence the way in which communication is executed and decisions are made. It can also influence how transgressions from the common norms are judged and dealt with; it can define or influence working hours and how, when, where and with whom information, office space and meals can be shared.

The planner needs a working knowledge of the cultural basis, values and norms of the company in which is a project takes place. The planner should be able to discern the relevant implications of these cultural aspects for the project, take these into account in the approach and periodically review them.

Measures

- Knows and recognises the values, norms and cultural requirements of stakeholders
- Knows, acknowledges and understands the implications of cultural values, norms and requirements for project planning

- Works according to the demands and cultural values of its stakeholders without compromising their personal values

1.5.2 Align the project with the formal culture and corporate values of the organisation

Description
All projects need to be aligned with the values of the organisation and have to follow the formal cultural rules and demands of related functional departments or support units and the culture of superordinate projects and strategy decision-making bodies. Sometimes the espoused values are written down in one or more documents (for instance mission statement, quality policy, or corporate values).
The planner should be able to discern the relevant implications of these cultural aspects for the project and take these into account in the approach. Moreover, the planner needs to be sure that the project supports the sustainable development of the organisation, which also includes corporate social responsibility (CSR).
CSR is a lever of control in complying with legal and non-governmental regulations, professional standards and other ethical and international norms. Through CSR an organisation encourages a positive impact on its activities on the environment, consumers, employees' communities, stakeholders and all other members of the society.

Measures
- Acknowledges and respects the organisation's formal standards and requirements
- Knows and applies the values and mission of the organisation
- Knows and applies an organisation's quality policy
- Acknowledges the implications of standards, guidelines, corporate values and mission, quality policies for the project
- Acts sustainably by practising cooperate social responsibility

1.5.3 Assess the informal culture and values of the organisation and their implications for the project

Description
All projects are linked to an organisation (or more than one) with its own informal culture. While the formal aspects of the organisational culture can have a significant influence, many more aspects also influence an organization's culture or subcultures. These include its architecture, furniture, dress codes, office jokes. Assumptions are deeply embedded, usually unconscious behaviours, such as the way people address and treat each other (including subordinates and managers), our problems and challenges are dealt with and tolerance for mistakes or irregular behaviour, all resulting from the history and cultural background of the organisation, its employees and its management. The planner should learn and analyse the cultural basis of the organisation for an in which the project takes place. The planner should be able to discern the relevant

implications of these cultural aspects for the project and take these into account in their approach.

Measures

- Technologies, analyses and respects the informal culture and values of the organisation
- Identifies the implications of the organisation's informal culture and values on project planning
- Adheres to the organisation's informal values and standards

3 Practice Competence Elements for project planning

The practice competence elements deal with the framework within the core activities and duties of the project planner. They are specific to the project planner competence baseline, although derived from the ICB4 "practice" competences.
The 13 practice competences are:

3.1 Project Planning Design and Requirements
3.2 Project Planning Organisation, Information and Communication
3.3 Contracts and Project Delays
3.4 Project Scope, Deliverables and Structure
3.5 Project Scheduling
3.6 Project Time and Milestone Management
3.7 Project Resource Allocation
3.8 Project Resource Optimization
3.9 Monitoring Project Progress
3.10 Planning Risks and Opportunities
3.11 Planning Steering and Control
3.12 Planning Stakeholders
3.13 Change / Transformation Management

3.1 Project Planning Design and Requirements

Definition

This competence element describes how the needs, expectations and constraints of organisations are understood and put into perspective by the planner, in order to establish or review or maintain an overall design of project planning, ensuring the greatest probability of success.

Taking into account this input, the project planning design describes how tasks, human and material resources, financial means, stakeholder objectives, organisational impacts and changes, risks and opportunities, governance, product delivery, priorities and emergencies are considered in the way project planning is organized and managed. Project planning design should be reviewed or assessed periodically and, where appropriate, adjusted. Indeed, external factors and success criteria may change over time, and they might lose their relevance.

Purpose

The purpose of this competence element is to enable the planner to successfully integrate all contextual and social aspects and derive the best design for project planning success.

Description

Project planning design is about developing, implementing, and monitoring a planning approach that best serves the organisation's and the project's objectives. It encompasses all the formal and informal success factors that facilitate or hinder the organisation's objectives and the success or failure of the project at hand.

Project planning design includes consideration of purposes, governance, structures and processes, applicable norms and regulations, cultural aspects, and personal and group interests in the organisation and society at large.

The selection of a planning approach should consider lessons learned from other project plans within the organisation, industry or outside. The specificities of the project and its complexity also play an important role.

Project planning design takes into account a wide range of topics, such as governance and decision-making, communication and resources. They consider rules and standards, respecting the norms and cultural values of the organisation and wider society.

Aspects such as perceived benefits, motivation, communication needs, contract requirements from stakeholders should also be addressed. Those need to be analysed and their impact on planning should be assessed. The planner should contribute to the prioritization of project stakeholder requirements as these might have an impact on project planning.

The clear and distinct definition or review of project objectives, factors and criteria is a major requirement from the beginning and during the execution of the project. This activity results in a detailed plan at the most general level that will later be transposed into specific actions that should lead to the success of the project.

The approach chosen or reviewed also includes the management and control strategy. The structure reflects pace, balance and involvement, and provides direction according to the task elements and their place in the project.

The selection of a strategy and the structuring of the project must be carried out before moving on to the plan, organisation and execution of the project. In addition, during the life cycle of the project, the chosen approach must be regularly reviewed and adjusted as circumstances change within the project or in its environment.

Knowledge

- Key success factors
- Success criteria
- Quality
- Feedback
- Benchmarking
- Complexity
- Success of the project, programme or portfolio
- Success of project, programme and portfolio management
- Success of project planning
- Project, programme and portfolio management tools
- Styles of leadership
- Strategy
- Project triangle (deadlines, resources, technical performance)
- Progress management
- Organisational project design rules and methodologies
- Specific methodologies relating to the company and its environment
- Organisational model
- Theory of change

Skills / abilities

- Environmental awareness
- Systemic thinking
- Achieving results
- Improvement/consideration of feedback
- Structural tree
- Analysis and synthesis

KEY COMPETENCE INDICATORS(KCIs)

3.1.1 Define / review project planning quality and success criteria

Description

Success factors are the criteria that stakeholders use to assess and judge the success of project planning. These criteria can be both formal and informal.
Formal criteria address the stated objectives. Achieving these goals and objectives under the agreed-upon conditions (e.g., strategic objectives, tactical and operational objectives) is only part of successful project planning.
The informal criteria by which stakeholders evaluate the results are also important. These factors may include the real reasons why a project is initiated, sustained, thwarted, or terminated.

Success criteria also include interaction with the broader context:
- Personal or group interests that are influenced by project planning or outcome
- How project planning is supported
- Conflicts with other projects and programmes, activities, objectives, resources

The planner lists formal and informal success criteria for project planning. Indeed, it is important for the planner to consider informal criteria as well as formal criteria because they will significantly influence the willingness of stakeholders to support and cooperate with the project and thus directly influence its success.
The success criteria for project planning play a crucial role in defining the overall approach. For example, if the main criterion is scheduling quality, quality processes, quality reviews and quality assurance will play an important role in the chosen approach. This approach will differ significantly from a project where the focus is on time (speed of delivery) or budget.
Success factors are elements that planners can incorporate into their project planning to increase the likelihood of meeting the success criteria and achieving a positive outcome. These factors can come from very different sources and take different forms. They may relate to the use (or non-use) of specific tools, methods or techniques, the selection of appropriate resources, the organisational configuration, the timing of the project, the reporting, the means and styles of communication, the methods of quality control.
During each project, the relative importance of success factors and criteria may change due to contextual or social aspects and to the dynamics of the project itself. Therefore, the planner periodically checks and reassesses the reality and relative importance of the success criteria and, if needed, makes the necessary changes in the approach to achieving success. These changes may even include advising the organisation to end the project prematurely.

Measures
- Identifies, classifies, and evaluates the influences of each of the five Perspective competence elements relevant to success
- Recognizes and assesses both formal and informal influence
- Evaluates and prioritizes the success criteria for each of the five Perspective competence elements
- Identifies and evaluates both formal and informal success criteria
- Defines and uses relevant project planning success factors
- Conducts periodic relevance reassessments / reviews of success criteria

3.1.2 Analyse, apply, exchange project planning lessons learnt

Description
At the beginning of the project, the planner gathers lessons learned from the planning of previous projects (both from their organisation and from stakeholders, using benchmarking) and applies the relevant lessons to the planning of the current project planning.

Periodically and at the end of the project, the planner, together with relevant team and stakeholders, evaluates the results and gathers the lessons learned from the current project.
Lessons are shared within the organisation. The planner knows and uses the different methods and tools for disseminating feedback in the organisation (e.g., through the PMO, knowledge bases, intranet).

Measures

- Recognizes and collects lessons learned from the planning of previous projects
- Applies relevant feedback to current project planning
- Recognizes and uses research and benchmarking methods to improve project planning performance
- Identifies and shares lessons learned from project planning within the organisation

3.1.3 Determine complexity and interdependencies and their consequences on the planning approach

Description

To select an appropriate planning approach, the planner should consider the specific complexity of the project plan, particularly the complexity of the expected outcomes and/or the complexity of the project processes.
Complexity in planning can have many causes and sources:

- The internal outcomes or processes required for the project may be innovative, technically complex and/or closely interconnected
- The project may involve teams, people, large number of suppliers, thus creating multiple interdependencies
- The project context may be complex, for example when several stakeholders have different interests or when there are many interfaces with other processes, projects, programs
- Timelines may be short, budgets limited, outcomes critical to the organisation

A comprehensive analysis will take into account the 10 criteria of the IPMA grid to characterize complexity.
All these internal and external factors must be considered by the planner, as they play an important role in defining an optimal strategy for the project.

Measures

- Identifies the level of complexity of the project by applying appropriate methods, including the 10 criteria of the IPMA grid
- Recognizes aspects that increase the complexity of planning
- Identifies and defines the impact of project-specific processes, constraints or outcomes on planning complexity
- Identifies and evaluates the impact of external and internal project parameters on planning complexity
- Evaluates and applies measures to reduce planning complexity

3.1.4 Identify / review the overall planning approach

Description

At the very beginning of the project, the planner chooses / reviews the overall planning approach with the highest probability of success, considering contextual constraints and demands, the complexity of project planning, return of experience, success criteria and available success factors.

This planning approach may include a vision, broad principles and a structure for planning in order to achieve success. It may include an overall definition of the scope, quality aspects, organisation, communication, documentation, planning and stakeholder approach, resource selection, risk tolerance, management and performance criteria.

The planner reviews this approach periodically, because contextual and social influences may change over the course of the project lifecycle.

Measures

- Evaluates the various possible planning approach
- Selects / reviews a planning approach for the project that is most likely to lead to success
- Explains and defends the chosen approach and its relationship to the success of the project
- Explains the main effects of the chosen planning approach on the project organisation
- Explains the main effects of the chosen planning approach on the organisation of the company
- Periodically re-evaluates the chosen planning approach based on contextual and internal developments
- Modifies the planning approach as needed and explains why

3.1.5 Define / review and analyse the impact of project stakeholders needs and requirements on the planning approach

Description

Identifying planning stakeholders needs and requirements requires knowledge of and communication with the permanent organisation, customers and end-users and any other key stakeholders.

Needs are not the same as stated requirements. Often needs are not formulated because they are obvious. Needs to be translated as much as possible into requirements. Expectations are very often hidden and unconscious but may prove extremely important to the project success. The planner should know enough about the stakeholders' interests and influence to be able to make this analysis.

After analysis, the planning requirements, needs and expectations have to be documented and prioritized. Priorities are made using criteria defined with top managers and external stakeholders.

The project plan execution should take this analysis into account.

Criteria for priorities may be related to:
- Contract
- Quality
- Organisation
- Communication
- Documentation
- Risk tolerance

Measures
- Knows the difference between needs, expectations and requirements
- Identifies and documents planning stakeholder needs and requirements
- Prioritizes planning stakeholder requirements using relevant criteria
- Ensures the consideration of stakeholder requirements on planning

3.1.6 Select and review the overall project plan execution

Description
Based on the chosen planning approach, the planner drafts, defines and structures the general organisation of the project plan. The overall plan will be detailed later through specific plans, but the basic design considers only the essential choices, such as make-or-buy, cascade or iterative cycle, internal or external resources, selected tools and methods, and the consequences of each choice for the success of the project plan. These choices made by the planner also include the best way to manage project plan. Successful project planning is an essential element and a prerequisite for the success of the project. In some cases, this can lead to choosing a planner with strong competence. In other cases, it will lead to a "first among equals" planner who can bring the team or stakeholders together. Often, this choice will vary depending on the circumstances and environments and/or the phase of the project.
Within the project, the planner periodically evaluates the overall project planning organisation, taking into account the progress of the project, changing contextual influences and demands, success criteria and available success factors. This often leads to changes and sometimes major modifications in the established structures.

Measures
- Defines and structures the overall planning organisation
- Periodically assesses the overall planning organisation of the project
- Modifies the overall planning organisation as needed

3.2 Project Planning Organisation, Information and Communication

Definition

This competence element addresses definition/review, implementation and governance of the project planning processes, related roles and responsibilities (involving hierarchical line management and project planning stakeholders). It also includes creation, organisation, storage and communication of data and documents related to project planning.

Purpose

The aim of this competence element is to enable the planner to define and implement an efficient temporary planning organisation, also taking into account the inseparable link between the organisational structure and the information and communication processes.

Description

This competence element describes how the project planning is organized. The organisation covers roles, responsibilities and mandates of the participants at the different levels of project planning. It also considers the human resources involved and the associated communication processes. It describes the formal flow of information, so that each organisation can take responsibility for the planning assigned to it and make decisions based on good information.
The planner is responsible for the quality, speed and flow of information.
Internal information, communication and documentation are closely linked to the management of the organisation and include the identification of needs, necessary processes, information infrastructures and control of the flow of internal and external information.

Knowledge

- Organisational Models
- Project relationships and hierarchical structures
- Work breakdown structure (W.B.S.), and related project planning organisation
- Information and communication systems
- Document Management Systems
- Information plan
- Communication plan
- Regulatory Requirements
- Information Security

Skills / abilities

- Participant involvement and assertiveness
- Setting up the organisation
- Delegation of tasks
- Management of interfaces with other parts of the organisation
- Use of project management software
- Database organisation
- Use of project management software
- Information and Communication Management Planning
- Document preparation techniques

KEY COMPETENCE INDICATORS

3.2.1 Define / review stakeholder needs related to project planning organisation

Description

An appropriate governance framework and structure must be put in place for project planning. Within this framework, roles and responsibilities should be clearly defined, decision-making authorities and levels of delegation should be identified.

Measures

- Considers the needs of stakeholders in the organisation of project planning
- Considers the responsibilities and needs of the different key members of the project team about the organisation of project planning
- Identifies links and interfaces with entities in the permanent organisation
- Identifies and records the respective roles of the organisation's functional departments and project managers

3.2.2 Define / review project planning structure, roles and responsibilities

Description

The planner may structure the temporary organisation of planning in a variety of ways, considering contextual characteristics such as governance and strategy, structures and processes, power and interests, norms and regulations, culture and values.
The technologies applied, the solutions chosen, the skills required, and the geographic location will also have a significant impact on the development of the organisational structure for planning.
The planner knows the advantages and disadvantages of different structures and is also able to define, recruit or participate in the recruitment of staff and set up a temporary planning organisation.

Measures

- Knows some basic methods for structuring a temporary organisation
- Applies a RACI type of approach to clarify responsibilities
- Designs and develops a governance framework adapted to the structure
- Sets up a temporary planning organisation

3.2.3 Implement, monitor and maintain project planning organisation

Description

The planner organises project planning, including the implementation, monitoring and maintenance of the temporary organisation. Implementation involves making the initially defined organisational structure operational, adapting processes and culture when required.
Management of planning organisation also includes changes in the organisation as the project evolves. Changes in contextual factors, such as strategy and/or decision-making authority, may affect the temporary organisation of planning and require modifications or simple adjustments.
By paying constant attention to the project environment, the planner can anticipate necessary changes in temporary planning organisation.

Measures

- Implements an appropriate project planning organisation
- Manages the project planning organisation, including stakeholder roles
- Adjusts project planning organisation as needed, including stakeholder roles

3.2.4 Define / review stakeholder needs related to project planning information and communication

Description

The planner knows the close relationship between information and planning organisation. Information needs can also determine the need for specific organisational structures. For example, outsourcing organisations with one or more offshore teams need a particularly efficient information system. Care must be taken to decide who gets or delivers what information. Overloading teams with too much information should be avoided.
In principle, stakeholders should only receive the information they need and in an appropriate format. The planner should identify formal and informal information/ documentation needs. Knowledge of company's structures and processes automatically includes knowledge of some of the formal information and documentation (specifications, plans, budgets, reports).
It is the responsibility of the planner to ensure that the information and requirements of the organisation are clearly defined and documented.

Measures

- Assesses and formalizes information and communication needs related to project planning
- Assesses and formalizes documentation needs related to project planning
- Establishes the various formal and informal information and communication channels

3.2.5 Establish / review infrastructure, process and systems for project planning information and communication flows

Description

The planner knows how to establish information and communication processes, considering roles and responsibilities and all applicable rules and guidelines in the organisation. Where necessary, appropriate systems and methods are implemented to supplement internal procedures.
A key success criterion is to remove and/or limit redundant information to establish effective information processes. The information must also be consistent and unambiguous. Information infrastructures cover the systems, means and methods required for the documentation, storage and communication of internal information. Infrastructure and information processing are inseparable in a high-performance organisation.
Therefore, it is essential for the planner to know these systems, their implementation and the information processing policies of companies.

Measures

- Explains the purpose and content of information and communication processes related to planning
- Communicates internal information through a variety of methods
- Ensures that redundant information is limited and/or eliminated
- Explains the benefits of different types of meetings
- Explains what is covered by an information and communication infrastructure
- Establishes planning and control mechanisms (e.g., documentation of key decisions)

3.3 Contract and Project Delays

Definition

This competence element covers the consideration of contracts by the project planner as well as the identification of the causes and effects of possible delays during the project.

Purpose

The purpose of this competence element is to enable the planner to consider all the provisions of the contract and to take them into account or transpose them into the deliverables structure (PBS), used as a starting point for the project work breakdown structure (WBS). It is also to allow the planner to analyse the delays of the project from different approaches including the analysis of project data, critical paths, cause and effect diagrams.
The customer contract defines the conditions under which a company (the service provider) undertakes, to perform for a customer, a mission or a specific work, for a fee. The missions carried out within the framework of a customer contract can be various:

- Material services
- Manufacturing and installation methods
- Intangible or intellectual services (consulting, events, communication)

The customer contract describes the object and the characteristics of the services, to frame the obligations of the provider, by indicating the means to implement and the expected result.
Subcontracting is an organisation of the distribution of the tasks of project by which a company entrusts to another company whole or part of a project to be carried out. It can be studies, production or services.
Subcontracting can be decided to call upon specialties missing in the company, or which must be reinforced in case of insufficient qualification or availability of resources. It allows a temporary increase of the resources assigned to the project.
Subcontracts are usually formalized in a document called “subcontract” or “agreement” mentioning the provisions agreed between the client and the subcontractor.
The contracts usually mention the following points (non-comprehensive list):

- The purpose of the contract
- The price of the service
- Payment deadlines and/or penalties for late payment
- The modalities for amending the contract
- Delivery terms
- Delivery (location, risks), transport, packaging
- Control and receipt of services
- Intellectual property

- The dates of conclusion and effect of the contract
- Place of jurisdiction and applicable law

Description

This competence element describes how the planner should be involved in the drafting and validation of contracts, then discern the elements of contracts that impact planning and then include these into the project planning.
It also describes how the planner should analyse project delays in order to accurately identify the causes of the delays. These analyses must be triggered as soon as delays are detected to avoid contract adjustments or the resulting litigation.

Knowledge

- Procurement Regulations
- General conditions of works contracts
- Types of management required according to the contract
- Standard contracts
- Supplier Relationship Management
- Payment management
- Penalties
- Dispute Management
- Cause-to-case diagram
- Critical path analysis methods

Skills / abilities

- Verification of the completeness of the contracts with respect to planning
- Validation or participation in the validation of contracts
- Experience of the elements of the contracts having an influence on the planning
- Negotiation of the elements of the contracts having an impact on the planning

KEY COMPETENCE INDICATORS

3.3.1 Contribute to the contracts drafting and validation

Description
The planner must participate in the drafting and validation of contracts and ensure that the elements necessary for project planning are fully described in the contract documents.
Those aspects can affect:

- The description of the purpose of the project from which the data useful for establishing the structure of the deliverables will be extracted (PBS)

- Time management data, including milestones, date or deadline constraints, end objectives, specific schedules
- Resource data, mainly associated with workloads and costs

Measures
- Participates in the drafting and validation of contracts
- Identifies contract data related to the description of project deliverables
- Identifies contract data related to the management of deadlines and key dates
- Identifies contract data from resource and cost contracts
- Identifies contract tasks that can be directly considered in the project's WBS

3.3.2 Review contracts and propose / include contractual obligations in schedule model

Description
When the contract is validated, the planner must include all data having an impact on the plan into the databases used for the project plan. These databases are mainly the following:
- Configuration Database: Deliverables Database (PBS)
- Database associated with W.P. or tasks
- Database associated with resource characteristics
- General databases: Calendars, units of time, charges and costs

Measures
- Transcribes the contract elements that impact planning into the databases required for planning
- After planning, identifies contract elements that need to be adjusted or clarified

3.3.3 Communicate different schedules and related comments

Description
Each type of schedule gives different information according to user's needs. There are usually several types of schedules:
- General project schedules
- Detailed project schedules
- Subcontractor schedules
- Customer plan
- Financing schedules
- Material assignment schedules
- Hardware maintenance schedules

Although all these schedules are usually established from common databases, the planner's mission will be to define and consider the needs or levels of information intended for each stakeholder.

In a context where project management systems are used, the publication of the results expected can be completely or partially automated.

Measures

- Defines the types of schedules and the desired information in relation to the stakeholders
- Implements the output of schedules according to the expressed needs
- Uses project management software features to automate scheduling delivery

3.3.4 Organize / implement project delay analysis

Description

The purpose of this indicator is to determine the causes of project delays and to weight these causes to determine the significant origins. For this purpose, the planner uses the most relevant among the available data that may result from different methods:

- Methods of comparison between forecast and actual plan (As Planned versus As Built - A.P.A.B.)
- Delay analysis using the window method
- "Collapsed As Built" delay analysis
- Cause-and-effect diagrams (Ishikawa)
- Analysis of planning results including critical paths, sub-project critical paths and task floats values
- Analysis of significant deviations from the results of measures of physical advancement. Global deviations can be sorted or filtered according to the RBS resource axis and/or the WBS project axis to determine the origins

A complementary analysis of Gantt charts, simultaneity and task floats allows in most cases the qualified and quantified determination of causes.
This approach is therefore based on planning results elaborated at a sufficient level and established in accordance with good practice.

Measures

- Knows project planning methods, including the physical progress method
- Knows the use of cause-and-effect diagrams and uses them
- Uses planning results, especially those from the Gantt Chart to determine the causes of delays
- Knows pros and cons of schedule delay analysis methods and organizes schedule management strategy accordingly. These methods are:
- As Planned versus As Built Analysis
- Windows Analysis (Contemporary period analysis)
- Retrospective Time Impact Analysis
- Understand contractual delay responsibilities and entitlements to claim, provides concurrent delay analysis and support prioritization and strategy to collect evidence

3.3.5 Audit and analyse subcontractors' schedules

Description
The quality and conformity of subcontractors' planning is an important factor to succeed in project planning. The audit and analysis of subcontractors' schedules is a management principle that aims to:
- Check the ability of the subcontractor to meet the planning requirements of the client
- Check the conditions under which the planning is carried out, especially in terms of validation of planning data and results
- Check the consistency of the planning with the project planning
- Check the conditions for synchronizing schedule updates

Validation of PBS and WBS as well as resource/time relationships are important points of the subcontractor planning audit.
The audit of subcontractors' schedules can take place at different stages:
- Selection of a subcontractor
- Assistance to the subcontractor in case of difficulties
- Modification of the schedule

The audit of subcontractors is also an opportunity to progress in the relationship between contractor and subcontractor.

Measures
- Plans and organizes planning audits of project subcontractors
- Validates the conditions for establishing subcontractors' schedules
- Validates the consistency of subcontractors' schedules with project schedules
- Writes a planning audit report

3.4 Project Scope, Deliverables and Structure

Definition

This Competence element defines the purpose and the content of the project. It describes the achievements, the results, the expected benefits and also the work necessary to produce them. It also deals with the limits of the project, notably describing formally or by omission what is not part of the project scope.
The structuring of the project consists in describing in tree form, therefore organisational charts:

- The organisation of the content and deliverables that define the purpose of the project (Product Breakdown Structure - PBS)
- The organisation of work packages and project tasks (Project Task Flow Chart - Work Breakdown Structure - WBS)

These two distinct representations therefore describe on the one hand the organisation of deliverables: Achievements, results, expected benefits (PBS) and on the other hand the organisation of the work necessary to produce them (WBS).
These representations consider in real time the evolutions of the project and integrate all the modifications identified as the project progresses.
Project structuring is often described as the first step in project planning. It also corresponds to the first data entry to be performed by the planner when a project management software is used.

Purpose

The purpose of this competence element is to enable the planner to understand the content of the project and to manage it, as well as to understand how it affects the decisions concerning the management and execution of the project.

Description

This competence element covers the process of understanding, defining and managing the specific content of the project, taking into account what is outside the scope of the project. It is therefore necessary to precisely define project boundaries, which are often crucial for understanding and decision-making about what is part of the project and what is excluded from it.
This competence element covers the definition of project deliverables, the establishment of the project's task breakdown structure, the definition of work packages and tasks. It also includes ongoing management of the project configuration. Configuration tracking and control can, in some cases, reduce the risk of goals creep. Most projects operate in a dynamic environment and, therefore, the scope is not fixed. To assure the permanent organisation that there is no drift, the planner controls the

project scope and content through continuous updating and monitoring of the needs, desires and expectations of key stakeholders, especially the customer.

Knowledge

- Hierarchical and non-hierarchical structures
- Definition of deliverables (content and exclusions)
- Breakdown structure of deliverables or project object (PBS or Nomenclature in the case of management of manufacturing / production operations)
- Organisation chart of Project Tasks (WBS)
- Work package (W.P.)
- Relationship to Cost Organisational Charts (C.B.S. or Cost Flowchart)
- Work package planning
- Configuration Management
- Data collection methodologies (scenarios, history)
- Knowledge and use of project management software features associated with the capture and management of PBS, WBS, W.P. and Tasks

Skills / abilities

- Definition of a product breakdown structure (PBS)
- Criteria for breaking down a project
- Definition of a work breakdown structure based on the most suitable division criteria for the project (WBS)
- Definition of a cost breakdown structure (C.B.S.)
- Use of a WBS glossary
- Configuration Management
- Practice of project management software features associated with entering WBS, W.P. and Tasks
- Planning of deliverables

KEY COMPETENCE INDICATORS

3.4.1 identify / review project deliverables

Description
Project deliverables are tangible or intangible assets (services, products) that constitute the results of the project. These are the measurable results validating the conformity of the project results to the objectives or requirements. The deliverables produced as part of the project are intended to be delivered to a customer (internal or external). The hierarchy of objectives covered in the competence element "requirements and objectives" is deepened and completed. The project outcomes resulting from the objectives are represented in a tree-like decomposition called "Product Breakdown Structure" (PBS)

The project deliverables and sub-deliverables are at the most detailed level of the priority scale. If a graphical representation is used, links can be highlighted between the objectives and the corresponding deliverables.

Measures

- Knows and uses goal prioritization
- Considers the organisation's existing project planning procedures
- Considers standard PBS if they exist
- Knows and explains the difference between goals, deliverables and tasks
- Organizes associated goals and deliverables
- Defines project deliverables and represents them as PBS
- Knows the principle of interactions between PBS and WBS
- Verifies the completeness of the PBS from the results of the WBS and vice versa (Consistency)
- Uses Agile software for structuring deliverables when using Agile planning methods

3.4.2 Structure project tasks and milestones

Description

Structuring project tasks and milestones entails a systematic division of the project into subsets called Work Packages, tasks, and milestones. A graphical presentation of the WBS is typically a tree structure with a number of stepwise divided sub-levels depending on the desired level of details of task or work elements. WBS

Just as the definition of PBS serves as a starting point for the definition of WBS, the definition of WBS will generally lead to the refinement and verification of the elements of the PBS. A task that would not result in a PBS does not have to be included in the WBS. Conversely, an element of the PBS that would not lead to the identification of a set of tasks or a task to obtain it does not have to be included in the PBS There is a permanent interaction between these two approaches throughout the life of the project.

For example, a task "establish the file of industrialisation remarks" of the WBS will necessarily result in a "file of industrialisation remarks" element in the PBS and vice versa.

Contrary to production management methods which use the principle of a quasi-definitive and validated nomenclature as the definitive support for data management, the PBS and the WBS will generally be subject to simultaneous adjustments throughout the project lifecycle.

Different criteria can be used to structure the WBS:

- One criterion that can be used is to ensure that the overall structure of the WBS reflects all the phases necessary to deliver the results of projects such as analysis, design, development, testing
- Another approach may reflect the different functional or physical structures of the project objectives

- A third approach may take into account the structure of the organisations or stakeholders involved in the project at the first or intermediate levels

Other structuring approaches, especially those related to resources in a small project context, can be used.
A WBS will generally use several decomposition criteria according to the levels:
Example: Phasing at the first level, organisations or stakeholders at the second level.
The WBS will consider interface tasks allowing the relationship with tasks from other projects (Project Portfolio) or external to the project.
One or more WBS codifications adapted to the project structure will be defined.
They will be used for sorting and filtering (Selection) data and results as well as for articulating the WBS with the cost breakdown structure.
An iterative (Agile) approach can be used to clarify and structure the project, although the level of detail obtained is usually not as detailed as with a sequential or linear approach.
In the case of project portfolios, the structuring will consider the interactions between projects.
Whatever the approach, the structuring of tasks in a WBS is, an essential means of obtaining an overall view of the tasks required to complete the project. It sounds like the nomenclature of a product.
The absence of the PBS or the WBS is a first indicator of inaccuracy in the project description.

Measures
- Considers the organisation's existing project management procedures
- Considers standard WBS if they exist
- Knows and explains the purpose and benefits of structuring project tasks
- Knows the uses of a WBS
- Knows and applies the principles of creating a WBS
- Knows the different decomposition criteria that can be used to build the WBS
- Knows the purpose and principles of coding a WBS
- Explains the consequences of the differences between the construction rules of a WBS
- Explains the limitations of the project and can give examples
- Arguments why and when a detailed WBS may be inappropriate when applying Agile methods to project management
- Uses project management software for entering WBS data and formatting results

3.4.3 Define or identify project work packages

Description
Depending on the level of detail chosen, the elements at the lower level of the WBS represent tasks or work packages with well-defined limits. The boundaries that can be considered well defined are:

- The overall success criterion of an effective work organisation structure
- The possibility of defining the data that characterize the task or Work package of tasks (duration, resources)

The definition of a work package or a task mainly includes (non-comprehensive list):
- The summary description of the work to be carried out
- The objectives of the work package in terms of identifiable result in the PBS
- The WBS coding
- The defined duration or the dates of execution
- Resource allocations
- Workloads and/or costs

If the duration, cost and/or resource requirement are not yet defined, they should be provisionally replaced by estimates to be confirmed later.
Work packages associated with their codifications can be grouped into control accounts for reporting purposes.

Measures
- Defines work packages
- Explains the purpose and benefits of work packages
- Explains how to define a work package
- Describes tasks
- Explains and justifies the data associated with the tasks
- Uses project management software to enter data for work packages or tasks and format the results

3.4.4 Organize the integration of different project schedules

Description
The various schedules involved in the project plan are derived from the stakeholder organisations whose planning system, practices, skills and means may be very different. The objectives of integrating the different levels of planning contributing to the overall planning of the project will therefore lead to the objective of harmonizing planning methods for the planner.
However, the planner will seek to achieve this objective of harmonization while preserving the practices of each of the stakeholders. Changing their practices too quickly or too abruptly could cause damages to the project in the short-term. This harmonization may be the subject of a specific project plan, possibly managed by a PMO or central planning services. This harmonization will therefore be carried out progressively along different axes:
- Harmonization of workflows
- Reliability of schedule
- Definition of the milestones necessary for the synchronization of schedules
- Harmonization of resource structures
- Harmonization of progress management methods

- Common coding rules
- Common rules for editing documents
- Standardization of units
- Implementation of computerized management systems able to integrate and consolidate the different levels of stakeholder plans
- Establishment of consolidated dashboards

Measures
- Defines or participates in the definition of integration objectives to be achieved
- Defines or participates in the definition of the harmonization objectives to be achieved for integration
- Plans and implements the action plans necessary to achieve these objectives
- Implements or participates in the implementation of the means, in particular IT resources, necessary for the integration of various levels of stakeholder plans
- Consolidates and validates the results of the integration of different levels of plans

3.4.5 Contribute to establish and manage project configuration

Description
Configuration management minimizes gaps, errors, and unforeseen changes to the project. Configuration management is intended to assure:
- That deliverables are aligned with stakeholders needs and requirements
- That all stakeholders assigned to the project work with the same version(s) of the project product

Projects take place in a dynamic environment where changes occur and changes or adjustments must be detected and managed, instead of being treated as obstacles that hinder the success of the project.
Managing a configuration is characteristic of an iterative, value-driven approach, instead of being planning- or task-oriented. Configuration management is an ongoing process.

Measures
- Defines the product configuration(s)
- Manages or participates in the management of the product configuration(s)
- Participates in the development of configuration management roles and responsibilities
- Aligns configuration dependency with the overall project goal

3.5 Project Scheduling

Definition

This competence element covers the modelling of the sequencing or linking of project tasks to verify the project process or progress as well as the feasibility and optimize its execution. This phase of the planning process is also called "Project Logic Analysis".

Purpose

The purpose of this competency element is to enable the planner to sequence and optimize the flow of all tasks required to produce the agreed-upon project results.

Description

Most project tasks depend on the completion or availability of results or the prior completion of other work packages or tasks. Based on these known dependencies or order relationships, a task sequence must be defined.
The scheduling method usually recommended and used by almost all project management or scheduling software tool is called the network scheduling method, which is the preliminary phase of the P.E.R.T. method. It has integrated some evolutions since its creation in the middle of the twentieth century. This method is notably validated by the scheduling functionalities made available to users of project management software tools.
Moreover, it is often discussed in the literature as an independent scheduling method, whereas it is an essential intermediate link between:

- Upstream: The description of the project resulting from the PBS and the WBS
- Downstream: The generation of schedule planning and planning elements to identify project and sub-project critical paths as well as to assess and control risks of delay

In a manufacturing management context, the sequence of operations on a workstation is driven by the essential procedure prepared and validated by the methods managers. This illustrates the absolute necessity of a schedule prepared by the planner. The knowledge, understanding of the stakes and skills of the planner concerning this aspect of planning must imperatively be validated if we wish to avoid a "relegation" of this tool whose necessity and validity are no longer to be demonstrated.
The objectives of project scheduling are mainly the following:

- To represent the course of the project, the sequence of tasks or W.P. considered as tasks
- To check the continuity of the sequence of tasks from the beginning of the project (example: Expression of needs) to the end of the project (example: Final receipt)
- To verify by looping the completeness of the WBS and therefore of the identification of thc deliverables in the PBS Introduce in the PBS and the WBS the complementary tasks identified during the schedule analysis

Knowledge

- Network Scheduling Method (PERT Programme Evaluation and Review Technique - Project Flowcharting - ADM: Arrow Diagramming Method - PDM: Precedence Diagramming Method)
- Different forms of network (Activities-On-Arrows or Activities-On-Nodes)
- Different types of connection or order relationships between tasks
- Data relating to links or order relationships
- Network Analysis
- Removal of non-immediate predecessors
- Network optimization and simplification
- "Start" and "End" Milestones - Network Closure
- Creation of milestones required to integrate the project into a portfolio of projects or to synchronize it with stakeholder schedules
- Milestones
- Spiral/iterative/agile development process

Skills / abilities

- Establish the list of tasks or W.P considered as tasks from the WBS
- Defines the tasks and work packages that are considered tasks
- Defines dependencies (Predecessors - Successors)
- Considers the interactions between projects in the case of a project portfolio.
- Establishes the dependency summary table
- Checks the consistency of the dependency summary table
- Calculates task ranks
- Sequence tasks
- Builds the network (Activities-On-Arrows)
- Scans the network and removes non-immediate predecessors (Redundant Links)
- Optimizes the network (simultaneous or concurrent engineering and parallelization of tasks with the objective of reducing the time to project implementation)
- Simplifies the network
- Uses project management software for task or Work Package data entry and results formatting

KEY COMPETENCE INDICATORS

3.5.1 Identify links between tasks or W.Ps. and create the tasks network

Description
The conditions of execution of each task are analysed. Thus, the list of all the tasks triggering each task's execution, called antecedents or predecessors, will be identified. Depending on data available, this list can be completed by a second list of tasks that can start after its completion, called successors.

In most cases and despite all the attention paid by the planner to the establishment and validation of the PBS and the WBS, this phase may lead to supplement the W.B.S with the new tasks identified. This necessity is due to the introduction of an additional transversal and sequenced analysis of the task list. On average, it is estimated that about 10% of tasks will be added to the WBS following this sequencing phase, which can be considered as the equivalent of validating a routing in production management. Due to the additions made to the W.B.S, it will also result in a more precise description of the PBS and therefore a minimization of forgotten tasks and deliverables.
All the sequences associated with each task will be consolidated in a summary table from which the execution ranks of the tasks will be calculated. The result of this calculation of the ranks will allow, by using the appropriate methods, to trace the network manually or to trigger the tracing of the network if a project management software is used.

Measures

- Determines for each task or W.P. the Predecessors / Upstream constraints
- Determines for each task or W.P. the Successors / Downstream constraints
- Verifies that the newly identified tasks or W.P. are taken into account in the WBS and therefore in the P.B.S
- Identifies the types of links different from Finish/Start links on the network (Start/ Start, Finish/Finish, Start/Finish links, and possibly leads and lags on the links)
- Draw up a summary table of the dependencies
- Calculates from this summary table the "ranks" of the tasks that will serve as input data for the network plot
- Uses a project management software tool to automate the drawing of the network from the summary table and the consideration of elementary scheduling

3.5.2 Verify the tasks network

Description

The network will later be used as a data carrier, for all plan calculations.
It is therefore important at this stage of planning to perform several checks. If these checks are not carried out, it is very likely that the plan obtained will contain errors whose causes will be more difficult to determine:
The main controls to be carried out are as follows:

- Presence of a Milestone at the beginning of the project
- Presence of an End-of-Project Milestone
- The network must be closed, which means that all tasks or W.P.s must have at least one predecessor or one successor, although this check is not comprehensive
- Absence of loops
- No redundant links
- Presence of external milestones related to plan integration or multi-project plan

These checks can be carried out in several ways:

- Either directly from the analysis of the task entry table and their precedence relationships (Predecessors + Successors)
- Either by proofreading the network obtained at the end of the process

Some checks are automated by project management software, but others are not.
For example, checking the plausibility of the process described by the network. This is obviously the responsibility of the planner.
The automation of scheduling calculations masks possible errors linked to data entry or erroneous units. The planner must check the consistency directly on the network.
Since no synthesis of the network is possible, this phase is based on a detailed analysis, which is key for the subsequent success of the plan.

Measures

- Controls the network links/relationships obtained from the schedule calculations
- Checks the general structure of the network
- Checks for lifecycle milestones or external connections (Plan Integration - Project Portfolio)
- Checks the plausibility of the network obtained (Project process)
- Performs format adjustments allowing easy reading of the scheduling result

3.5.3 Verify consistency of project tasks network and WBS

Description

The WBS describes the structure of the WPs and the tasks of the project. Its completeness depends on the level of precision with which it has been established. A WBS established from a standard WBS or a life cycle procedure validated by feedback will provide superior guarantees to a WBS established as part of an innovative project or weak stakeholder experience.
Scheduling imposes the modelling of the sequence of tasks, therefore guarantees and validates, whatever the context, a sequence of tasks in accordance with their definition.
At this stage, the planner will check the consistency between the level of definition of the tasks in the WBS and their inclusion in the scheduling

Measures

- Knows the interactions between planning methods (Scheduling to WBS and PBS - Scheduling to Time Management)
- Verifies that WBS includes network tasks or WPs
- Verifies that PBS includes all associated deliverables

3.5.4 Optimize the tasks network

Description

Once the consistency of the list of tasks or W.P. considered in the network and the content of the WBS have been verified, it remains necessary to optimize the network.

This optimization aims at reducing the delay and can be carried out by using different means in a concurrent engineering perspective, which can be the following:

- Parallelization of tasks traditionally performed in series
- Using task overlap methods (leads associated with Finish-Start links)
- Integration of milestones for network simplification

Measures

- Knows the principles of concurrent or simultaneous engineering
- Analysis and criticism of the schedule obtained
- Applies task overlapping techniques
- Knows and uses the features of project management software associated with link types and delays

3.6 Project Time and Milestone Management

Definition

This competence element covers the identification and positioning of all the tasks of a project in relation to a time line in order to predict and manage their execution. This phase of the planning process is sometimes referred to as "Quantitative Project Analysis".

Purpose

The purpose of this competence element is to enable the planner to:

- Establish the provisional schedule of execution of the tasks: Project Timetable, Gantt chart, Linear chart
- Determine the expected duration of the project
- Identify critical tasks and critical path
- Determine task floats: Free floats, Total floats, Negative floats, essential results for the determination of the delay risks
- Identify tasks whose duration needs to be precisely estimated
- Identify tasks that can be moved or whose duration can be adjusted due to resource levelling or smoothing
- Evaluate delay-risks
- Sub-project critical paths
- Sorting tasks by increasing float values
- Interpret the potential consequences of task postponements on the overall schedule
- Have the information needed to manage priorities and reduce lead times
- Establish the baseline schedule

Description

The goal of time management is to determine which tasks need to be completed when, and to optimize the project execution.
For projects, tasks are analysed, sequenced and planned over time and their execution is visualized in a schedule. They are assigned to people or teams to be executed in the right order and at the right time.
Time management also covers the monitoring of variations. Deviations in project execution, whether caused by external influences (changes in requirements or deliverables, unavailability of resources or lack of funding...) or internal (late or out-of-specification deliveries...) may require a new schedule.
Periodically, the planner will compare the actual schedule to the baseline and make the necessary adjustments. With iterative planning, the schedule can be divided into phases of a certain duration. At each iteration, a certain sequence of activities (e.g., design, execution, testing, and commissioning) can be defined.

The overall project planning then focuses on the number of iterations and other activities (preparation, follow-up). In case of uncertainty about the time required for a particular phase or activity, an additional duration or a float can be introduced into the schedule.

Knowledge

- Types of schedules
- Planning based on durations
- Planning based on workloads and resource availability
- Methods for estimating task duration
- Probabilistic analysis
- Calculating the average duration of a task
- Duration units
- Early schedule
- Late schedule
- Identification of critical tasks
- Identification of sub-project critical tasks
- Calculation of free and total floats
- Construction of the Gantt Chart
- Construction of the Linear chart
- Planning modes
- Early scheduling
- Backward scheduling
- Consideration of end targets, negative floats
- Milestones
- Calculations associated with link types and leads/lags
- Critical path analysis
- Methods to reduce time line
- Baseline planning
- Spiral/iterative/agile development process

Skills / abilities

- Performs all the necessary calculations to build the Gantt Chart
- Builds the Gantt chart
- Identifies project and sub-project critical paths
- Determines task floats
- Considers the time constraints imposed on the project
- Uses "Gantt Chart" features of project management software

KEY COMPETENCE INDICATORS

3.6.1 Estimate / review task durations and dates necessary to manage project milestones

Description

The list of tasks needed to achieve the agreed outcomes is usually defined from an analysis of the deliverables (PBS) and/or requirements, preferably through a WBS For each task, the time frame required for completion must be determined. This may include prior determination of the resources in skills and availability for each task.
However, in a context of uncertainty, the determination of durations and resource data remains an essential prerequisite for the preparation of the Gantt Chart and is based on the preparation of estimates.
Different estimation methods for project areas can be used. In all cases, the results obtained must be validated by the estimates derived from the planner's competence in the area of activity concerned and by the estimate of the person in charge of the W.P. or the task.

Measures

- Knows the difficulties of estimating durations, workloads, and availabilities
- Knows the effects of uncertainty on planning and what needs to be done to minimize its effects
- Estimates the projected durations and workloads of each W.P. or task in case of uncertainty
- Estimates the projected durations and workloads of each W.P. or task in relation to its responsible and/or experts
- Uses estimation methods associated with the project area of activity
- Calculates the average values of durations from a probabilistic analysis
- Uses project management software features associated with taking estimates into account
- Knows the orders of magnitude of the durations or loads for the trades concerned

3.6.2 Consolidate task durations and dates necessary to manage project milestones

Description

The calculations required for the planning of the project, and in particular for drawing up the Gantt Chart(s), assume that the durations are defined for all the WPs and tasks. The planner's main task at this stage is to define and/or collect the data associated with the task durations or the load/availability ratios of the resources needed to calculate the durations. When several material and human resources are available, a balance must be found between quality, cost and time. This balance depends on the criteria and requirements for the success of the project.
The "business" competence of the planner will be essential at this stage to validate the commitments or estimates of the project stakeholders. With iterative planning, the

planner simply defines the duration or workload data associated with the tasks required for the deliverables expected in the current iteration.

Measures
- Defines the units of durations adapted to the project
- Defines or reports on the calendar durations of tasks
- Defines or considers workloads, availability and allocation rates of resources
- Calculates task durations based on resource workload and availability
- Validates and negotiates, if necessary, duration commitments or workload and availability data with stakeholders
- Uses project management software to enter duration or workload data associated with tasks

3.6.3 Make calculations necessary to manage project milestones

Description
Once all the forecasted durations have been determined, either directly as calendar durations or from a resource load/availability ratio, it is possible to perform the calculations required to draw up the Gantt chart.
These calculations are carried out according to a process to provide the start and finish of the tasks as well as their floats. They are supported by the previously established task network. This network is they only way to consider scheduling data.
The use of project management or scheduling software tools is essential at this level as soon as the project involves a high number of tasks. It is also the way to reduce the risk of errors.

Measures
- Performs the earliest possible schedule calculations from the task network
- Determines the possible duration of the project
- Calculates early and late dates from the task network
- Determines critical path
- Performs float calculations
- Determines sub-project critical paths
- Uses project management software tool to perform calculations to obtain schedule results and/or plot the Gantt Chart

3.6.4 Build the project Gantt chart

Description
The Gantt Chart is the most common representation of a project schedule.
It allows the direct reading on a single support of the main results of the project plan:
- Task start and end dates
- Floats
- Project and sub-project critical paths

- Order relationships (Linked Gantt chart)
- Structuring the project by summarizing lower-level tasks (Folding-Unfolding)

In practice, the tasks of the Gantt Chart will most often be classified according to the W.P. but can be classified according to other criteria: distribution according to the stakeholders concerned for example.

Measures
- Draws the Gantt Chart
- Differentiates on the Gantt Chart the different types of tasks: Critical, sub-critical, non-critical
- Indicates the types and values of floats on the Gantt Chart
- Plots the durations of the W.P. from the synthesis of the task plan synthesis
- Plots links between tasks (Linked Gantt Chart)
- Checks with links, float types and values, the consistency of the Gantt Chart
- Verifies the plausibility and accuracy of critical paths
- Uses project management software to edit the Gantt Chart

3.6.5 Analyse and optimize the Project Gantt Chart

Description
Many tasks depend on the availability or prior completion of other work packages or tasks. Based on these dependencies and the duration set for each activity, time range for each task can be defined.
At this stage, the planning of the main milestones of the project can be checked. In particular, the critical and sub-projects critical paths can be determined. The detailed analysis of these critical or sub-projects critical paths makes it possible to determine a first set of actions to be considered to meet the project's deadline constraints.
This first set of actions will be completed during the resource analysis, before establishing the final Gantt Chart.

Measures
- Identifies the tasks that make up the project lead time (Critical and sub-projects critical paths)
- Negotiates or re-estimates critical task durations to meet project time constraints
- Identifies possible new critical or sub-projects critical paths
- Updates the Gantt Chart until it complies with the project's master schedule or deadline targets
- Uses project management software to perform the necessary simulations

3.7 Project Resource Allocation

Definition

This competence element includes the structuring, definition, allocation, control of the resources that are necessary for the execution of the project.
Resources include the people, equipment, materials, infrastructure, tools and other assets needed to carry out project tasks according to objectives.
This competence element encompasses the definition of a strategy for allocating and using resources for the best progress of the project.

Purpose

The purpose of this competence element is to enable the planner to ensure that the necessary resources are allocated as needed to achieve the objectives.

Description

To achieve the objectives, a project uses resources. Resource management means applying an appropriate approach to defining, obtaining and allocating these resources. Resource allocation should be carried out during the forward planning phase and should be constantly monitored and adjusted throughout the project lifecycle.
The planner must ensure that resources are available on time and in sufficient quantity, that human resources have the necessary skills and that they receive the information, means and training necessary to carry out the required tasks successfully.
Given the huge amount of data processed, the competence indicators include the ability to use and implement computerized tools which are key for resources and deadline's management
Since resource requirements and availability change regularly, both for controllable and uncontrollable reasons, resource management is a permanent and regular process.
In the case of projects, the planner often must negotiate with the permanent organisation or external service providers in order to obtain the desired resources.
Some unforeseen event can occur such as insufficient funding, progress problems, equipment failures, climatical events, labour disputes. They may reduce the availability of certain types of resources and lead to conflicts. Thus, these conditions may require rescheduling of tasks and replacement of resources assigned to current or future activities, especially if critical tasks are affected by such events.
Procedures should therefore be in place to identify such contingencies and ensure that necessary adjustments are made as soon as possible.

Knowledge

- Definition of resources
- Assessment of resources

- Resource Breakdown Structure RBS
- Data associated with resources
- Methods of resource allocation: Uniform or non-uniform allocations
- Types of resource allocation: Fixed rate - Fixed workload - Fixed duration
- Consequences of simultaneous allocations of the same resource
- Calculating resource utilization
- Workload histograms
- Consideration of resource availability
- Critical chain

Skills / abilities

- Creates resource request plan, allocation plan and management
- Develops the Resource Competence Matrix - identification of competences and documentation of gaps in individual competences
- Prioritizes and allocates resources, based on multiple divergent priorities

KEY COMPETENCE INDICATORS

3.7.1 Contribute to / review the strategic definition and structure of project resources

Description

Resource management is based on considering the relationships between tasks or WPs previously identified in the project WBS and the resources likely to be allocated to the project or project portfolio (RBS).

Once the resource strategy has been defined or taken into account, the description of the resources and associated data is usually carried out using a hierarchical structure called a resource breakdown structure (RBS)

This RBS is most often a subset of the organisation's general organisation chart, limited to the resources that can be used by projects. It can also be the result of the consolidation of the resource organisational charts of the project stakeholders. This RBS can constitute a database of the organisation managed by the Human Resources Direction or the PMO In this case, it will only be used by the planner for resource allocation.

In the case of less structured organisations or smaller projects, the RBS can also be established directly by the planner using internal databases of the project management software.

The RBS typically uses a decomposition criterion related to the hierarchical structure of the project's stakeholder organisations. However, other decomposition criteria can be considered, especially in the case of dedicated project teams.

The RBS generally supports one or more codifications allowing the sorting or filtering of data or results according to a resource axis and /or stakeholder organisations.

Measures

- Reviews and analyses the organisation's resource mobilization capabilities and identifies trends and associated preventive or corrective actions
- Identifies the resource requirements of the project
- Defines or participates in the definition or upgrade of the resource database considering the resource needs (RBS)
- Verifies, completes, and uses the existing resource database if this is the case
- Defines or participates in the definition of the codifications associated with the resource database (RBS indexes)
- Uses or participates in the use of project management software to define and manage the structure of resources

3.7.2 Define or contribute to the definition of data associated with project resources

Description

The planner must characterize the resources. They are described in the RBS and can be assigned to project tasks.
Resources mainly include people, equipment, materials, infrastructure, tools, non-financial assets or services.
The data associated with resources can be extremely numerous. Project management software manages very detailed data with automated processes. The main data are as follows (non-comprehensive list):

- Description of resources
- Resource Competences
- Indicators of competence
- Types of resources (Personnel, equipment)
- Availability of resources
- Cost of resources
- Calendars associated with resources
- Default resource allocation rate
- Unit costs in the case of material resources or services

Some specific characteristics must be considered when allocating human resources, such as productivity or learning speed which may vary from individual to individual.

Measures

- Defines or participates in the definition of the characteristics of the resources identified in the RBS and potentially assignable to the project
- Defines or participates in the definition of data associated with resources
- Defines or participates in the definition of resource calendars
- Verifies pre-existing calendars
- Uses or participates in the use of project management software to define and manage data associated with resources

- In the case of a pre-existing resource database under the responsibility of the HRD or PMO, validates or verifies the data associated with the resources potentially assignable to the project

3.7.3 Identify or take into account potential resources and negotiate their availabilities.

Description
Once the required resources have been defined, the appropriate resource providers must be identified.
Resources can come from the organisation or from third-party suppliers. Many organisations impose rules for the acquisition of resources. When the planner faces the question “make or buy”, they must rely on existing formal and informal networks.
A good knowledge of the organisation, as well as a general overview of the market is necessary to identify and decide on supply alternatives. Obtaining external resources is very different from allocating internal resources. While mobilizing internal resources involves only issues of quality and availability, the cost of external resources must also be considered and negotiated.

Measures
- Contributes to “make or buy” decisions
- Contributes to creating and evaluating supply alternatives
- Contributes to defining a procurement strategy
- Participates in negotiations with suppliers

3.7.4 Allocate resources to project WBS

Description
Resource allocation is an essential part of project planning. It associates the resource(s) needed to each task. This operation allows forecasting, monitoring, control and management of resources, their results and the corresponding costs.
For this phase of project planning, it is therefore necessary to:
- Create links between the tasks defined in the WBS and the resources identified in the RBS
- Define for each link created the quantities to be used, usually referred to as «Assignment Rate” or “Workload”

Assigning resources is therefore closely related to project planning, because the simultaneity of assignments or task overlays can lead to resource overloads and thus either to an adjustment of assignments or to a change in scheduling with the aim of eliminating conflicts.
Changes in the schedule and changes in the quality and availability of resources therefore have a reciprocal impact.
After identifying these resource requirements, the planner defines when resources should be available, their quality and in their quantity. This can result in one or more

detailed resource workload plans. The resources allocated to the project must be distributed within the project according to needs and according to the strategic resource plan. The conditions under which resources have been allocated must be respected.
When there are divergent resource needs, the planner should consider all options and find the best way to manage those needs based on priorities, urgency, or other relevant criteria.
Measures to overcome resource shortages must be developed and implemented. The planner must be able to organize the distribution of resources and adapt it if necessary. This applies not only to the resources for which the planner is directly responsible, but also to the resources to achieve project objectives that are under the responsibility of other parties (in accordance with the strategic resource plan).

Measures

- Challenges the quality and quantity of resources required for each task in the WBS
- Assigns or verifies for each task in the WBS the allocation of resources necessary for its implementation
- Defines or verifies for each task in the WBS the allocation rates or amounts of resources allocated
- Completes or arranges for the completion of database for unidentified needs
- Negotiates or participates in the negotiation of resource conflicts

3.8 Project Resource Optimisation

Definition

The competence element for optimizing, levelling and smoothing resources includes the control and validation of resources required to complete the project.
It includes optimizing the use of resources within financial and time constraints and monitoring and controlling them on an ongoing basis.

Purpose

The purpose of this competence element is to enable the planner to ensure that the necessary resources are available as needed to achieve the objectives.
It also includes the alignment of resource assignments and the preliminary Gantt Chart of the project, while respecting the required skills and availability.
In most cases, this consistency will lead to a reconsideration or adjustment of the preliminary schedule established at the outset in the absence of taking into account the simultaneity of the assignments. These adjustments will become even more important in an integrated plan environment or in project portfolios for which final plan can only be validated after considering all assignments.

Description

Many interactions between resource data and time data require a project management software to make these data consistent and to edit the results of the forecasting.
In an environment of limited resources, no other calculation tool can be considered. The absence of such a tool capable of managing the complex matrix of intersections WBS – RBS at this stage of planning probably indicates very inadequate management of resources as well as approximate time management.

Knowledge

- Histograms of workloads per time unit
- Availability of resources
- Levelling
- Smoothing
- Establishment of the final Gantt Chart
- Workload forecasts by time unit
- Cumulative cost forecasts (Planned Value: PV - "S" curves - Budgeted Costs of Work Scheduled - - B.C.W.S.)

Skills / abilities

- Essential use of project management software for the definition and allocation of resources as well as for the automated smoothing and levelling
- Edition of the final Gantt charts
- Edition of final cost and workloads forecasts

KEY COMPETENCE INDICATORS

3.8.1 Analyse use of resources and take / propose corrective actions

Description

As resources have been allocated to all tasks, it is possible to measure the total workloads per time unit or load histograms for each resource and to compare these forecasted workloads with the available resources.

Levelling or smoothing operations may result in increasing the project timeline. Before using them, it is important to carry out an initial analysis phase relating to the definition and correct allocation of resources. If necessary, the planner must take corrective measures. In the case of abnormal overloads or underloads, assignments must be checked.

The planner must also regularly assess the quality and availability of the allocated resources. If resources are external, discussions with suppliers and other contractors may be necessary to improve the availability of resources or to replace them.

Resource performance can also be improved. The resources concerned may benefit from specific development, coaching, and training measures. This needs to be negotiated and coordinated with resource providers.

The planner is responsible for the allocation and reallocation of key resources, including resources out of his direct responsibility but which contribute to the success of the project.

Relevant indicators need to be put in place and monitored to ensure the proper use of resources. This systematic analysis measures the difference between forecasted workload and resources availability.

Measures

- Defines a systematic approach to assess the projected resource workload
- Reviews load plans or time unit load charts for each resource
- Proposes and negotiates adjustments of loads and availability
- Offers opportunities to improve skills and know-how
- Contributes to resolve a skills gap with the relevant team member and superiors

3.8.2 Perform levelling and smoothing operations and finalize the project plan

Description
Resource availability is generally limited. At the end of the assignment phase, the project planner must plan the execution of the tasks based on resources availability.
In addition to reviewing the quality and quantity of resources, two methods can be used to make resource allocations compatible with their availability:

- Resource levelling, which can lead to an increase in the projected project duration as well as changes in critical paths and floats
- Resource smoothing, to use the resources in the most uniform way by re-arranging tasks within their floats

Project management software automates the implementation of multi-project - multi-task - multi-resource algorithms using these methods and is the only way that can be used as soon as the number of projects, tasks and resources become large.
However, the planner checks the resource workload plan and ensures that the results provided by their algorithms are consistent. At this level, project resource planning is like similar to production resource planning.

Measures

- Identifies by using workload plans or resource histograms the list of resources overloaded
- Implements levelling and smoothing operations, verifies and takes into account the results with regard to critical paths, task completion times, project completion time
- Uses project management software to perform the necessary levelling and smoothing
- Checks the compatibility of the final planning with the project master planning
- Disseminates and validates the final schedule (Baseline schedule)

3.8.3 Establish workload and cost forecasts

Description
At this stage of the planning, the necessary resources have been allocated to all the tasks and the forecasted project plan can be considered as definitively established. It is therefore possible to establish a certain number of forecast indicators by cumulating charges and costs.
These indicators can be established for the overall project or separated according to project subsets and/or resource structures using the WBS and RBS codifications.
The forecast indicators are generally as follows:

- Histograms of resource loads per time unit, which can be associated with availability curves
- Histograms of costs per unit of time of the resources
- Budgeted and cumulative cost of planned or scheduled work (S-curve: B.C.W.S. - Budgeted Cost of Work Scheduled - or PV - Planned Value -)

Measures

- Contributes to defining and organizing the project's forecasting dashboard
- Integrates the load and cost forecasts into the dashboard, considering the forecasting and monitoring needs expressed
- Checks the conformity of the load and cost forecasts with the objectives

3.9 Monitoring Project Progress

Definition

This competence element includes:

- To take into account the conditions of progress of the project
- To measure any deviations from baseline plan
- To maintain the project schedule reliable throughout its execution phase

Purpose

The purpose of this competence element is to enable the planner to track and control all the elements necessary to produce the agreed results of the project.

Description

As soon as the baseline plan is validated and the tasks are initiated, control systems (such as progress meetings and time spent recording systems) must be put in place. Various methods, such as the earned value method, based on considering the increase in value as the project progresses (Earned Value Management - E.V.M.), can be used to measure progress against objectives.
A project schedule can be subject to many disruptions, resulting in necessary adjustments. These can have various origins (changes in deliverables and/or requirements, modification of the nature of the tasks or their characteristics, planned or unavailability of resources or financial means, late or out-of-specification deliveries.) and can lead to new plan. Periodically, the schedule must be compared to its baseline and, if necessary, updates should be made.

Knowledge

- Project performance measurement benchmarks
- Different methods of to measure progress
- Weighted-start-and-finish Method
- Method 0/25/50/75/100
- Expert judgment Method
- Unit-of-work method
- Remainder to do method
- Milestones Method
- Earned value method (E.V.M.)
- Indicators for monitoring progress by costs
- Physical progress
- Schedule or cost progress rates
- S-Curves in cost (Planned value PV - B.C.W.S.)
- S-Curves in progress rate (Earned value - EV)

- S-Curves in actual costs (or workload) (Actual Cost AC - Actual Cost of Work Performed - A.C.W.P.)
- Schedule variance (SV)
- Cost Variance (CV)
- Time variance (TV)
- Schedule performance index SPI = EV/PV
- Cost performance index (CPI = EV/AC)
- Estimate Cost At Completion (ECAC)
- Estimate Duration At Completion (EDAC)
- Budget to date
- To-complete
- Date line
- Broken line of progress
- Cost reports
- Dashboards

Skills / abilities

- Estimates, records, consolidates and validates the progress of project tasks in the appropriate format
- Uses project management software to enter progress data and obtain all results from data entered
- Analyses the consequences on project plan
- Formats and edits all the results for the project dashboard or in preparation for the progress meeting

KEY COMPETENCE INDICATORS

3.9.1 Measure, review and record project tasks progress

Description

The management of project progress is based on the identification and recording of data associated with project tasks:

- The percentage of physical progress rate (E.V.M. Method)
- The cost and workload progress rates.
- Percentage of completion by deadline

But also, data associated with corrective actions used to update plan documents:

- Re-estimated task durations
- Resource allocations and re-estimated workloads

Measures

- Determines the methods of measuring progress
- Determines how to update progress

- Defines, measures, estimates or takes into account the progress of tasks according to established rules
- Validates progress data if entered directly by stakeholders
- Considers new data on time and resources

3.9.2 Edit project progress indicators

Description
Standard benchmarks for measuring project performance are based on the Earned Value Management (E.V.M. method, which uses cumulative curves of costs and expenses weighted by the value of advancements.)
The main curves used are:

- Forecast cost (or workload) curves of work scheduled (BCWS - Budgeted Cost of Work Scheduled - or PV - Planned Value -)
- Budgeted Cost or Load curves of the Work Performed (EV) produces forecasted load curves (PV) and progress values
- Actual Cost or Workload curves (AC) directly derived from actual cost or workload measurements, or time spent on project tasks

Measures

- Periodically updates the cost or planned workload curves by considering the evolution of the project forecasts (PV)
- Periodically publishes the budgeted cost or workload curves of the work performed (EV)
- Periodically publishes the actual cost or load curves of the work performed (AC)
- Automate the edition of these curves from the planning and progress data using a project management software

3.9.3 Analyse variances

Description
The simultaneous edition of cumulative S-curves allows to identify a certain number of deviations at the date of the measures useful to characterize the overall situation of the project.
The main variances measured are:

- Schedule variance: Difference between planned value (PV) and earned value (EV)
- Cost (or workload) variance: Difference between actual cost (AC) and earned value (EV)
- The delay measured from the time difference between the forecast (PV) and the progress-weighted forecast (EV)

Measures

- Edits and disseminates variance indicators
- Interprets positive or negative values of deviations

- Identifies the cause of deviations using WBS and RBS filters.
- Calculates and integrates schedule and cost performance indexes into dashboards

3.9.4 Update the plan taking into account variances and make the necessary adjustments

Description
As soon as deviations are observed in the project, the planner will update the plan, considering their causes and revisions to the estimate durations and costs.
Most project management software tools automate that function. However, the planner must validate new data or hypothesis resulting from previous work.

Measures
- Applies adjustments to the schedule in response to variances
- Considers updates to durations and costs estimates
- Determines and analyses critical path and floats updates
- Initiates the necessary actions to ensure that the new schedule is consistent with the objectives
- Updates and validates in agreement the new baseline plan with the project manager

3.9.5 Establish the project progress report

Description
Progress reports (dashboards) provide information on the status of project plan (deadlines, resources, workloads, costs, risks and opportunities, tough points) in the previous and current phases and development forecasts for the current phase and until the end of the project.
Reports include periodic verbal and written updates on the status of project plan and forecasting. Information is transmitted by team members to the project manager and by the project manager to stakeholders (such as the organisation's management or the project board).
Progress reports also include financial statements and the results of project reviews. When the planner and/or team are highly experienced, it may be sufficient and acceptable for stakeholders to receive information only on the tough points. In this case, a report will only be issued if something significant needs to be reported rather than providing regular reports on the status of project plan.

Measures
- Makes a hierarchical structure of plan (what, when, how often, how)
- Reports on the project progress
- Reports on the plan forecasts
- Reports on phase changes

3.9.6 Contribute to the making of the project final report

Description
The project final report reconstructs the history of the project and its progress against the forecasts.
It usually includes the following chapters:

- Description of the project in all its aspects
- Selected solutions
- Last update of the schedule
- Last update of the cost and workload dashboards
- Organisational aspects
- Project results

Measures

- Contributes to the development and drafting of the end-of-project report
- Takes into account or has taken into account the elements resulting from the feedback of the planning

3.10 Planning Risks and Opportunities

Definition

This competence element includes identifying, analysing, assessing, planning, and implementing actions related to the risks and opportunities associated with the planning activity that may alter or enhance the ability of project plan to achieve its objectives.
Risk and opportunity management helps the planner make informed choices, prioritize actions, and distinguish between different action plans. Risk and opportunity management is an ongoing process that takes place throughout the project lifecycle.

Purpose

The purpose of this competence element is to enable the planner to effectively understand and manage the risks and opportunities related to planning, including processes, overall strategies, action plans and their adaptation during the project.

Description

Planning risks (negative effects) and opportunities (positive effects) related to planning are always considered according to their correlation and their consequences for the achievement of project planning objectives. It is recommended in the first step to consider which overall strategies will best serve the corporate and project strategies. After that, the planning risk and opportunity management process is characterized by a first phase of identification and evaluation, followed by the development of action plans to deal with the identified risks and opportunities. Action plans must be developed and implemented in accordance with the overall risk and opportunity strategies.
The planner supports the participation and engagement of team members in the process of managing risks and opportunities and the involvement of other relevant stakeholders or experts whenever necessary.
The risks and opportunities are mainly the following:

Risks in the project development phase:

- Weak planning skills
- Poorly defined specifications and project processes
- Consistency of the WBS and unverified deliverables leading to deliverables that do not comply with the specifications
- Failure to consider feedback from similar projects carried out previously
- Exchanges of information distorted by stressful situation of planners or actors due to objectives, management or the client
- Insufficiently defined responsibilities of tasks
- Inaccurate job descriptions

- Lack of definition or precision of the data associated with the tasks: durations, human and material resources
- Work packages that are insufficiently detailed and interpretive
- Insufficient definition or instability of data associated with resources: availability, calendars, holidays
- Failure to consider data associated with standards or regulations: safety, environment
- Undescribed scheduling resulting in the absence of validation of the WBS and therefore the PBS as well as the impossibility of identifying critical paths, floats; so, insufficient control of deadlines
- Failure to meet the agreed deadline due to insufficient planning
- Infinite capacity planning due to the lack of project management software capable of carrying out the levelling or smoothing essential for the resolution of resource/task conflicts within the framework of the project but also in the context of the planning of project portfolios
- Excessive or insufficient plan of resources
- Unexpected changes in planned resource allocation
- Underestimation of the project budget
- Identification of additional costs as the project progresses
- Lack of planning updates: coordination or progress meetings
- Planning function insufficiently taken into account or integrated into the organisation of the project
- Planning function not understood and not recognized
- Insufficient training of planning staff
- Insufficient integration of vertical and cross-cutting plan levels
- Lack of project management software, the only computer tool capable of managing all the data necessary for planning and implementing the algorithms necessary for editing the associated results
- Software databases that are not up to date

Risks during project execution:

- Verification and updating of initial planning not performed
- Insufficient responsiveness of data entry systems, planning devices and tools generating unacceptable discrepancies between the image of the project resulting from planning and the reality of execution
- Dissemination of out-of-date or inconsistent execution schedules

Planning Opportunities:

- Setting up standard WBSs
- Definition of responsibilities associated with data entry
- Implementation of a document management system

- Implementation of a project management software
- Training of service managers in decentralized entry of advancements
- Writing planner function definitions

Knowledge

- Analysis of Strengths, Weaknesses, Opportunities and Threats (SWOT analysis) related to planning
- Exposure to and tolerance to plan risks and opportunities
- Causes of plan risks and opportunities
- Risk management strategies and planning opportunities
- Techniques and tools for identifying risks and opportunities
- Monte Carlo Analysis
- Decision Trees - ISHIKAWA Diagram
- Pareto's law (20 / 80)
- ABC (Activity-Based Costing)
- Failure Model - FMEA (Failure Modes and Effects Analysis) Method
- Eisenhower Matrix (Urgency / Importance)
- Forecasts of costs and durations
- Qualitative tools and risk assessment techniques
- Severity of risks
- Likelihood, probability or frequency of risks and opportunities
- Benefit of opportunities
- Criticality of risks
- Severity / Likelihood Matrix
- Sensitivity analysis
- Action plans and fallback solutions
- Response strategies and management plans for plan risks and opportunities
- Planning for possible scenarios
- Residual risks and opportunities
- Register of risks and opportunities

Skills / abilities

- Identification techniques
- Evaluation and prioritization techniques
- Development of action plans
- Implementation, monitoring and control of management plans
- Implementation, monitoring and control of global strategies

KEY COMPETENCE INDICATORS

3.10.1 contribute to / review the development of the risks and opportunities management process

Description

The planner participates in defining the risk and opportunity management process to ensure that risks and opportunities that impact the plan are managed in a consistent and systematic manner throughout the project lifecycle. The process should include defining the methods to be used to identify, analyse, evaluate, address risks and opportunities, and must take into account the organisation's risk and opportunity management policy, international and national standards, benchmarks and best practices.

The risk and opportunity management process defines the roles and responsibilities of stakeholders and defines the communication modalities.

When projects are part of a programme or portfolio, the risk and opportunity management process also describes the reciprocal impacts. The process of managing risks and opportunities should be integrated with the project management process and must be validated by management.

Measures

- Knowledge of the general project risk and opportunity management process.
- Identifies the different risk management methods and opportunities of this process.
- Specifies the process of managing risks and opportunities and ensures its integration into the overall project risk and opportunity management process.
- Verifies the compliance of this process with the organisation's policy and with standards and best planning practices.
- Ensures consistent application of the process of managing risks and opportunities.

3.10.2 identify / review and register risks and opportunities impacting the project plan

Description

- The planner is responsible to identify and consider all sources of risks and opportunities impacting the plan. The planner can use a variety of techniques and sources to identify risks and opportunities:
- Feedback from past planning projects
- Documentation
- Tree approach
- Creative sessions with team members, stakeholders and experts

Different sources of risks and opportunities have an impact on plan, both internal and external to the project. The sources of risks and opportunities impacting plan and

potential risks and opportunities will be recorded in a specific chapter of a list usually referred to as the "Risk Register and Opportunity Register".
Identifying risks and opportunities must be an ongoing process.

Measures

- Identifies and explains different sources of risks and opportunities
- Identifies and considers risks and opportunities
- Documents risks and opportunities
- Creates a register of risks and opportunities that impact plan
- Verifies that plan risks and opportunities have been addressed in a specific section of the project's risk and opportunity register
- Identifies potential responses to identified risks and opportunities

3.10.3 Assess / review probability and impact of risks and opportunities on the project plan

Description

The planner is responsible for the ongoing task of assessing the consequences of the identified risks and opportunities. The assessment of risks and opportunities must be done qualitatively and quantitatively. Qualitative assessment can cover a more in-depth analysis of the sources behind the risks and opportunities. It analyses each risk or opportunity and determines the level of severity or importance.
This phase leads to the establishment of a "Risk Assessment Matrix": Likelihood / Severity Matrix or to a prioritization of opportunities.

Measures

- Performs qualitative assessment of risks and opportunities
- Performs quantitative assessment of risks and opportunities
- Prioritizes risks in a risk assessment matrix
- Prioritizes the importance of opportunities
- Calculates the criticality of risks and opportunities

3.10.4 Define / review strategies and action plans to address risks and opportunities

Description

The planner is responsible for the ongoing process of defining and implementing optimal actions for each risk or opportunity. This process involves evaluating various possible types of actions by selecting the most appropriate ones to eliminate the effects of threats by reducing the likelihood of risk occurrence.
For each risk or opportunity, action strategies may include (non-comprehensive list):

- Eliminate risk through additional actions
- Protective actions to reduce severity
- Preventive actions to reduce the likelihood

- Avoid the risk or promote opportunity by deciding to reorient the activity concerned
- Accept the risk to foster an opportunity
- Accept the risk and make the associated cost and time provisions
- Accept the risk or opportunity following a reasoned and formal decision
- Eliminate the source of risk
- Re-evaluate the probability and severity
- Share the risk with a third party
- Transfer the risk to a third party being aware that the risk is not eliminated
- Prepare and implement, if necessary, fallback solutions

Risks not acceptable and opportunities to develop require appropriate treatment to manage a residual risk or opportunity. In the same way, the opportunities identified will trigger associated action plans.

Measures

- Explains various ways and methods for implementing a chosen overall strategy for the process of managing risks and opportunities
- Evaluates the actions related to risks and opportunities, including their strengths or weaknesses
- Defines actions related to risks and opportunities that impact planning
- Defines the means and methods for implementing an action plan related to the risks and opportunities
- Assigns resources with the necessary skills to implement actions and verifies their availability
- Communicates and implements action plans associated with risks and opportunities

3.10.5 Monitor evolution of risks and opportunities impacting the project plan

Description

Risks and opportunities that impact plan should be monitored and reassessed periodically. As new information becomes available, the severity and probability may change, and new risks and opportunities may arise. In addition, actions can be redirected. Global policies can also be changed.

The management of risks and opportunities is therefore not only a periodic process, but also a continuous one.

Measures

- Monitors and controls the integration into planning of action plans associated with risks and opportunities
- Updates action plans related to risks and opportunities
- Communicates updates to these action plans
- Updates the register of risks and opportunities as the project progresses

3.11 Planning Steering and Control

Definition

Based on the definition and structure of the project, all the elements are brought together in a project management plan, the execution of which is controlled by the planner. The plan must be regularly updated based on changes in the project or context. The control is regularly adapted and improved so that the planner masters the evolution of the project.

Purpose

The purpose of this competence element is to enable the planner to establish and maintain a balanced and integrated vision of project management. Maintaining balance, consistency and performance is crucial to achieving the expected results.

Description

This competence consists in gathering all the information necessary to prepare and to make these decisions. Many processes and activities are described in detail in the other competence elements.

In this element, the planner takes into account their combination, as stipulated in the project definition and structuring documents. The basic cyclical process is: organize, schedule, plan, execute, control, adjust the plan or modify the execution.

From a project management point of view, the objective is to master plan and follow-up. Information must be sought and integrated, the organisation and teams must be chosen.

The planner must determine how to plan and scale the project planning workload and how to manage the project. This includes participation in choosing the right management style, the extent of delegation (what and to whom to delegate). All this is defined in one or more steering documents (vision, roadmap, plan) that must be discussed and accepted.

Once the project is implemented, the control processes must be operational. These processes regularly gather information on progress, resource utilization against baselines, financial aspects, compliance with quality and other standards, stakeholder satisfaction. Regular reporting (both from performers to planner and from planner to stakeholders) is an essential part of these skills.

To continuously feed the learning process, the effort spent on project planning should also be evaluated on a regular basis and changes may be necessary.

A predefined and transparent change management process is another essential element in project control.

At the end of each phase of the project life cycle, an evaluation must take place and a report must be prepared, indicating the results obtained, the successes and the feedback.

Knowledge
- Phase/transition from one phase to another
- Dashboard and report
- Project Support Function (PSO or PMO)
- Deming cycle (plan, do, check, act)
- Change Request
- Management by objectives
- Exception handling
- Feedback reporting
- Planning for key phases/milestones
- Decisions on "make-or-buy"
- Exception report
- Problem Report
- Project Management Plan
- Project evaluation (end of phase)
- Discharge
- Decision-making power

Skills / abilities
- Progress meeting
- Change Management
- Earned Value Analysis
- Work progress curves
- Reporting
- Negotiating change requests
- Project Start-Up Workshop
- Kick-off meeting
- Closing meeting
- Problem Management
- Change Management

KEY COMPETENCE INDICATORS

3.11.1 Set up / review the management system to monitor project progress

Description
Project task progress measurements can be achieved in different ways:
- Measurement and recording of progress by task managers
- Measurement and recording of progress by specialized personnel
- Measurement and input at project updates or coordination meetings

The planner will have to, together with the project manager, define and implement the methods and means best suited to the project and ensure that they work properly

Measures

- Defines and implements the modalities of management of the progress of the projects
- Defines and proposes the progress dashboards best suited to the project
- Assures the updating and dissemination of these those dashboards

3.11.2 Contribute to the development / review of the project management plan

Description

The first phase of each project is essential, as it is the foundation of a successful project. This preparation phase is often characterized by uncertainty, with summary or not yet available information.
Stakeholders' requirements are sometimes only roughly defined, their expectations are sometimes unrealistic, and the deadlines requested are unachievable.
A proactive project management style, a well-prepared and effectively managed start-up workshop, and the recruitment of the right staff for the project team can improve the success of a project. One or more start-up workshops should focus on the development of the project charter and the preparation of the project management plan, defining the roles of the team. The planner participates in the preparation of the project management plan and plans the project. From the general design, the planner gathers, analyses, evaluates and prioritizes enough information from stakeholders and experts to refine this approach and contribute to the project management plan. This plan will be based on information and choices related to requirements and quality, expected deliverables and constraints, organisational and communication structures, necessary resources and budget, planning and main risks and opportunities.
Finally, the plan, the resources and the budget must be validated and approved, to launch the start-up and execution phase of the project.

Measures

- Participates in the organisation of the project start-up process
- Helps gather all the necessary information from stakeholders and experts
- Analyses, evaluates and prioritizes planning information
- Participates in the organisation of a workshop for the start of the project
- Participates in the preparation of the project charter or project management plan
- Participates in the preparation and communication of the organisational chart and load plan of the project management team
- Participates in the preparation and management of the transition from one project phase to the next

3.11.3 Initiate / review and manage / review the transition to a new project phase

Description
After the decision to fund and continue the project, the start of the next phase and all subsequent phases are carried out keeping in mind the following:
- The specific objectives of the next phase of the project
- All necessary organisational changes
- The need to confirm or amend the project charter and project management plan

The detailed schedule, resource allocation, budget, risk and opportunity register, and possible expected benefits (profitability analysis) must be updated.
Depending on the size or complexity of the project, a kick-off meeting is an effective way to engage and inform the project team about the plans, requirements, and objectives of the starting project or project phase.
This meeting or workshop can also be used to define work distribution, planning, assignments, or project values in more detail.

Measures
- Participates in the organisation of the management of the project execution process
- Participates in the definition of objectives and expected results of the following phases
- Manages the transition phase
- Participates in the organisation of a kick-off meeting

3.11.4 Control / monitor project performance against the project plan and propose corrective actions

Description
Control is based project objectives, plans and contracts. This management process measures actual project progress and performance, compares it against the baseline, and takes necessary remedial actions.
Control is normally done through checks against pre-set objectives by measuring results and correcting deviations (diagnostic control). When there are major uncertainties, these can be reduced by using feedback and suggestions from operational members to adjust the process (interactive control).
Control and reporting are carried out for the current period and includes a forecast for an appropriate number of future time periods. An integrated project monitoring and reporting system covers all project objectives, the corresponding success criteria for the relevant project phases and requirements of all stakeholders.

Measures
- Defines a schedule performance control cycle
- Describes means and methods applicable to performance control
- Measures progress and performance

3.11.5 Assess, obtain approval and implement changes to the project plan

Description

Changes are often necessary in a project schedule due to unanticipated occurrences. It may be necessary to change the project specification or the contracts terms with suppliers or customers. Changes must be monitored against the original project goals and objectives as set out in the business case and/or project charter.
At the start of the project, the change management process to be adopted should be agreed with all relevant stakeholders. A formal, proactive change management process that anticipates the need for change is preferable to a process that only reacts after the need for change is obvious.
A change to the scope of the project plan is made by a formal, predefined process. The change process embraces everything that results from the change required or new opportunity identified. It includes agreement on the change decision process, agreement on the need for change and the decision to accept the change and its implementation. This applies for all kinds of changes. Change management identifies, describes, classifies, assesses, approves or rejects, realises and verifies changes against legal and other agreements. Changes can be requested by any party and have to be managed as both proposed and approved changes, as well as properly communicated to all relevant stakeholders. For the management of a change, its direct and indirect effects on the whole project plan and its context are taken into account. The impact of the changes on the project deliverables, configuration, time schedule, cost, project plan, and financial risks and opportunities are determined by comparison with the project baseline. Once the changes have been accepted, the project plan is adjusted accordingly.

Measures

- Participates in the development of the project plan change management process
- Participates in the preparation of project plan variance or change reports

3.11.6 Contribute to the closure and evaluation of a phase or a project

Description

The close-out process takes place after the completion of the project or a phase of the project, after the results of the project or phase have been delivered. Each phase of a project or sub-project should be formally closed with an evaluation and documentation of the phase carried out, checking that objectives have been achieved and client expectations met. In the close-out of a phase, the proposals for the next phase of the project should be reviewed and any issues requiring a decision submitted to the appropriate body for authorization.
Where a formal contract has been signed, considerations include transfer of responsibilities from the contractor to the project owner, the commencement of the warranty period and the final payments that need to be invoiced. Handover documentation (also known as "as built") needs to be produced and training provided to

those who will use the project results. These are essential to ensure that the benefits of the investment made in the project are realised.
Project results and experience gained are evaluated and the lessons learned are documented so that they can be used to improve future projects. Project team members will be required for new assignments and should be formally released from their roles and responsibilities.

Measures

- Participates in the organisation of the close-out process of a phase of the project
- Participates in the organisation of a close-out workshop of a phase of the project
- Participates in the implementation of a comprehensive evaluation of the project
- Participates in the preparation of a 'lessons learned' report

3.12 Planning Stakeholders

Definition

This competence element includes identifying, analysing, engaging and managing the attitudes and expectations of all relevant stakeholders. Planners, groups or organisations participating in, affecting, being affected by, or interested in the execution or the result of the project plan should be seen as stakeholders. This may include sponsors, customers and users, suppliers / subcontractors, alliances, partners and also other projects, programmes or portfolios. Stakeholder engagement includes constantly revising, monitoring and acting upon their interests and influence on project planning. It can also result in the development of strategic alliances to build organisational capacities and capabilities where both risks and reward are shared.

Purpose

The purpose of this competency element is to enable the planner to identify and effectively manage stakeholder interests, influence and expectations.

Description

Stakeholder engagement is an ongoing process, throughout the project lifecycle. Stakeholders are the partners for and through whom the project planning will be successful. Stakeholders' expectations, needs and ideas form the basis for the project; stakeholders are the necessary contributors to the project in terms of money and resources; they are also the users of the project outcome.

Stakeholders come in various forms and groupings (higher management, users, suppliers, partners, operators, pressure and special interest groups). They have varying attitudes, influences, and interests. Therefore, each stakeholder or group of stakeholders has different information needs.

An engagement strategy (often laid down in a communication plan) is therefore essential. This strategy might be executed by setting up formal and informal communication channels, as well as more involving forms, such as alliances, collaboration or networks. Alliances are often documented and formalized through a contractual document such as an alliance contract, or through the creation of a joint venture entity. Employees often work in separate parts within an entity or may be part of one or more different organisations. Networks have no clear power structure, and hence are more difficult to engage with.

Changes in the stakeholder environment must be continuously monitored to ensure that objectives are met.

Knowledge

- Stakeholder interests
- Stakeholder influence
- Stakeholder Engagement Strategy
- Communication plan
- Collaborative agreements and alliances
- External environment scanning relating to social, political, economic and technological developments

Skills / abilities

- Stakeholders' identification
- Analysis of contextual pressures
- Demonstrating strategic communication skills
- Expectations management
- Formal and informal communication
- Good presentation skills
- Networking skills to identify potentially useful and opposite stakeholders
- Contextual awareness
- Undertaking conflict resolution

KEY COMPETENCE INDICATORS

3.12.1 Identify planning stakeholders and analyse their interests and influence

Description

The planner identifies all the people, groups, and organisations relevant to project planning. The planner must first analyse the attitudes of each of the stakeholders (individual or group) and identify the reasons for their attitude (interests in the outcomes or in the process of the project). Next, the planner must understand what beneficial or harmful effect (influence) this stakeholder (individual or group) can potentially have on the project planning.

Stakeholders' interests may come from different sources (for example, because they want, or must, use project deliverables or because they compete for scarce resources or budget). These interests can be large or modest, positive or negative. In the latter case, they reflect opposition to the project, for one reason or another. The influence of a stakeholder can be greater or less and can apply to one or more areas (such as being able to provide or deny funding, resources, office space and equipment, priority, access). The planner performs an analysis at the beginning of each project, identifying the stakeholders, their interests and influence. During the project, the planner maintains an active analysis of the project environment, to identify new stakeholders, changed interests or changed influences. These changes in the stakeholder environment may be the result of changes in the project itself (for example, moving from a design phase to an execution phase). More often, they are the result of changes in the context of the project (organisational changes, personnel changes in management, economic changes, new regulations). The planner analyses the relevance of these changes to project planning.

Measures

- Identifies the main categories of stakeholders in the project planning
- Identifies and qualifies stakeholder interests in the project
- Identifies and evaluates the influence of stakeholders
- Identifies relevant changes in or around the project
- Analyses the consequences of changes for the project
- Takes actions to manage project stakeholders

3.12.2 Develop and maintain a stakeholder strategy and a communication plan

Description

The planner will devise a stakeholder strategy: How to engage, keep informed, involve and commit the various stakeholders to the project plan, its strategy and its outcomes. This can be done by approaching each stakeholder (or group of stakeholders) differently, depending on their interests and influence. Stakeholders with similar interests and influence can be grouped together. The stakeholders' strategy is often laid down in a communication plan which describes for each stakeholder (or group) the why, what, when (and how often), how (through which communication channel), who (should communicate), and the level of detail of the communications.
The communication plan can be seen as a synthesis of the expectations of the different stakeholders so that they are aware of and adhere to the outcomes of the project (what and when) and are not disappointed due to overly high expectations of progress and results.
Each communication is at least two sided. So attention and care should be given to whether and how the sent communication was received, and follow-up should be given to feedback and other incoming communication.
As circumstances change, the communication plan should be regularly revised and updated. Potential alliances are developed, and potential collaborators are identified. The benefits and outcomes of a partnership or alliance are identified for all parties. A relationship is established and developed with potential collaborators.

Measures

- Highlights the importance of a stakeholder strategy for project planning
- Prepares a communication plan associated with project plan
- Adjusts the communication plan and/or strategy according to changing circumstances
- Explains the reasons for changing the communication plan
- Identifies and assesses opportunities for alliance and partnership in planning
- Identifies and evaluates potential collaborators

3.12.3 Collaborate with stakeholders to gain their cooperation and commitment

Description

For almost all projects, the most important stakeholders, include customers, executives and sponsors. Often the executive is the funder (budget) and/or can decide on resources, priority of needs, definition of objectives. With these primary stakeholders, managing expectations is of the utmost importance. The commitment and trust of the executive, higher management and/or sponsor(s) is of great benefit both to the success of the project and its management. A good working relationship and open communication should be established.

Sometimes a single person has several roles; most often different people fill one or more of these roles. They all have their own expectations, interests and influence on the project. Depending on the project, executive and/or sponsor can play a role in managing stakeholders and act as ambassadors, as they often have a status and connections that the project planner does not have.

For almost all projects, early and active user participation is a prerequisite for success. Users (or their representatives) can provide information on needs and requirements and indicate how the project outcome will be used. This is often essential to the definition of each of the deliverables. Users (or groups of users) can also provide resources.

Suppliers can bring resources, knowledge, and materials to the project. Care should be taken to select the best suppliers, especially if knowledge, resources (humans and/or materials) can only be obtained from outside the organisation and formal contracts must be established to obtain them.

Partners are individuals, groups or organisations that cooperate to jointly deliver a portion of the deliverables; they can also make a wider contribution to the achievement of the project's objectives. These partners may have joined forces for only one specific part, or they may work together on the basis of a broader alliance. Partners can also be other managers with whom it is necessary to develop the progress measurement or deliverables of the project in order to optimize the benefit for the organisation.

Where the project has a steering committee, one or more key users (user representatives) and the main suppliers (supplier representatives) may be part of this committee.

Users and other stakeholders can be part of a working group that advises the executive committee or steering committee. The planner needs to focus on these stakeholder groups early in the project and use their influence to select the right supplier and user representatives.

Measures

- Collaborates with the project organisation and the permanent organisation
- Collaborates with customers and users and involves them in project planning
- Involves suppliers in project planning
- Cooperates with partners to achieve optimal results for planning organisation

3.12.4 Organize and maintain networks and alliances

Description

As part of the stakeholders' strategy, networks and alliances can be implemented. These can be both formal and informal. When they are formal, agreements are negotiated and documented, and a cooperation plan is developed and implemented. As part of this plan, performance measures are identified, and an exit strategy is developed.

All networks and alliances should be evaluated frequently and improved when necessary. Alliances may be ended by design, or earlier if the relationship is no longer beneficial to the constituent organisations or stakeholders. Often, the organisation is quite likely to want to renew alliances with the same partners for new ventures in the future, so the ending of a formal relationship needs to be handled carefully.

Networks are more informal and tend to be sustained beyond the project lifecycle.

Measures

- Develops and implements a partnership plan associated with planning
- Implements satisfaction indicators associated with planning
- Follows up on key partnership agreements associated with planning

3.13 Change / Transformation management

Definition

Change can be defined as an improvement of the current situation considering the past. Transformation can be defined as a mutation to a new situation based on a vision of the future.

Purpose

The purpose of this competence element is also to enable the planner to help the companies, organisations and individuals around him to transform themselves, to reap benefits and achieve the expected goals.

Description

Transformation occurs when, based on vision, behaviour is changed because there is a will to do things differently. Transformation is vision lead and depends largely on the strength of the vision and the willingness of the people who share the vision to really put their energy into making it happen.
The level of change and transformation management required by a project will largely depend on the amount of disruption created in individuals and groups day to day lives come up plus attributes such as culture, value system and history with past changes. Change and transformation do not primarily happen by design and are not usually a linear process. The individual needs to regularly monitor and evaluate the effectiveness of the changes and adapt as a change or transformation strategy. The individual also needs to take into account the change capacity and capabilities of people, groups or the organisation in order to help them successfully adapt or transform.
Projects usually deliver new capabilities. However, it is only when these capabilities are put to use that value is added and benefits can be achieved. Organisational or business changes often affect or alter processes, systems, organisational structure and job roles, but most of all the influence people's behaviour. Changes can be quite small, or they can require a complete transformation sometimes, they can even be disruptive, which means special skills are needed to bring them about. In many cases, a project will induce an organised change but will have ended before the benefits resulting from it are realised.

Knowledge

- Learning methods for individuals, groups and organisations
- Organisational Change Management Theory
- Impact of change on individuals
- Personal change management techniques
- Group dynamics

- Impact assessment
- Stakeholder analysis
- Motivation theory
- Theory of change

Skills / abilities

- Assessing the capacity and aptitude for change of an individual, group or organisation
- Consideration of behaviour of individuals and groups
- Dealing with resistance to change

KEY COMPETENCE INDICATORS

3.13.1 Identify / review change / transformation requirements and opportunities

Description

For a business perspective-oriented projects, organisational requirements and the projects context are analysed to determine which transformation or business change needs to occur and when. For a more societal perspective-oriented project, to determine which societal groups can and should be influenced by the project. This can be done by interviewing, gathering knowledge, analysis of data and using workshops. Sometimes, opportunities arise because of changes in market conditions, the projects environment or other organisational or societal changes. Change requirements and opportunities will change regularly, so they need to be regularly reviewed and adapted.

Measures

- Identifies groups and individuals affected by planning-related change
- Maps group interests in planning
- Identifies change needs and opportunities regularly
- Adapts to changing interests and situations

3.13.2 Develop / review a change / transformation strategy

Description

A change strategy is developed by the planner (or emojis and therefore is put together by the planner) to address the envisioned changes or transformations. It will be based upon the intensity and the impact of the change and takes into account the ability to change or the willingness to transform of the organisation, society or people. The timing of changes to align with organisational or societal dynamics and opportunities also needs to be considered. The plan is developed through consultation and is regularly updated.

Learning, monitoring and assessing what works and what doesn't and in which situations, is part of the strategy. Changes and transformation do not happen overnight, but usually take a while before value is added.
When changes or transformations are more consequential, a stepwise approach is developed so that early successes can be valued and used as incentives for further change. Change plans can sometimes be planned and structured but can also be focused on group behaviours come on power, on learning, on emergence. There is no one right way to do change, but the planner needs to anticipate the change.

Measures

- Identifies societal, organisational and personal change or transformation strategies, recognising, for example, innovators, early adopters, the majority and laggards
- Collaborates with others to validate strategies
- Documents strategies in a general planning change plan
- Develops a step-by-step approach if necessary
- Regularly adapts the change or transformation plan to integrate feedback and the impact of changes on the project planning environment or in society
- Regularly adapts the strategy based on the success of the change and the benefits that flow from it

3.13.3 Implement the change / transformation strategy

Description

Based on this change strategy, a set of possible interventions is planned. This might include workshops, training, information sessions, pilots, serious games and visioning, but there will also certainly be interventions to be made regarding power and influence and handling resistance. Once a change is made, measures should be taken to sustain the change and to help organisations and individuals to avoid falling back into old behaviour.

Measures

- Design a consistent intervention plan
- Implements targeted interventions
- Leads or organizes workshops and training
- Addresses resistance to change
- Organises and implements mass media interventions
- Uses reinforcement techniques to ensure that the new behaviour is sustainable

www.ingramcontent.com/pod-product-compliance
Ingram Content Group UK Ltd.
Pitfield, Milton Keynes, MK11 3LW, UK
UKHW061657190726
13853UKWH00008B/2250